Art Essays

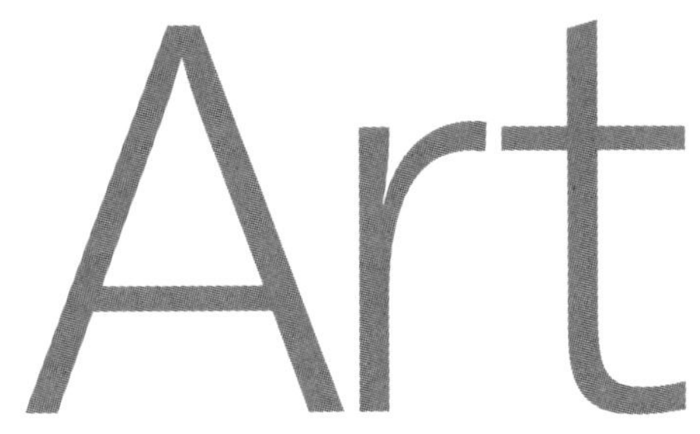

A COLLECTION

THE

NEW AMERICAN

CANON

The Iowa Series in

Contemporary Literature

and Culture

SAMUEL COHEN,

series editor

Essays

ALEXANDRA KINGSTON-REESE EDITOR

UNIVERSITY OF IOWA PRESS, IOWA CITY

University of Iowa Press, Iowa City 52242

www.uipress.uiowa.edu
Printed in the United States of America

Cover design by Trudi Gershenov; text design by Richard Hendel

Printed on acid-free paper

Library of Congress Cataloging-in-Publication Data
Names: Kingston-Reese, Alexandra, 1989– editor.
Title: Art Essays: A Collection / Alexandra Kingston-Reese, editor.
Description: Iowa City: University of Iowa Press, [2021] | Series: The New American Canon: The Iowa Series in Contemporary Literature and Culture
Identifiers: LCCN 2021012123 (print) | LCCN 2021012124 (ebook) | ISBN 9781609388119 (paperback) | ISBN 9781609388126 (ebook)
Subjects: LCSH: Art.
Classification: LCC N7443.A757 2021 (print) | LCC N7443 (ebook) | DDC 700—dc23
LC record available at https://lccn.loc.gov/2021012123
LC ebook record available at https://lccn.loc.gov/2021012124

Contents

The principle which controls it is simply that it should give pleasure; the desire which impels us when we take it from the shelf is simply to receive pleasure. It should lay us under a spell with its first word, and we should only wake, refreshed, with its last. In the interval we may pass through the most various experiences of amusement, surprise, interest, indignation; we may soar to the heights of fantasy ... or plunge to the depths of wisdom ... but we must never be roused. The essay must lap us about and draw its curtain across the world.

— VIRGINIA WOOLF, "The Modern Essay," 1925

Acknowledgments

That this book exists at all is in large part due to the conversations I had with Grace Sinclair when this book was only a whim. She encouraged me to make it happen, and most importantly saw what it could become. I owe a huge debt, too, to Lola Boorman, who generously read the draft and asked the sharp questions it needed. Thank you both for being, in equal measure, the ideal reader of the art essay.

My sincerest thanks go to all the authors who enthusiastically agreed to reprint their essays in this collection: Chloe Aridjis, Tash Aw, Claire-Louise Bennett, Teju Cole, Geoff Dyer, Sheila Heti, Katie Kitamura, Chris Kraus, Jhumpa Lahiri, Ben Lerner, Orhan Pamuk, Ali Smith, Zadie Smith, Heidi Sopinka, and Hanya Yanagihara. Not one was hesitant, and for that I'm incredibly grateful.

I owe immense gratitude to everyone at the University of Iowa Press, especially Sam Cohen, the editor of The New American Canon, for suggesting this book for the series. Meredith Stabel edited the book with incredible enthusiasm and kept me on schedule. Jacob deftly managed the permissions, and Richard Hendel made the essays come to life.

Hannah Roche, Nicoletta Asciuto, Shazia Jagot, Juliana Mensah, and Jane Raisch were the cheerleaders this project (and I) needed in the strangest of years. I'm immensely proud and grateful to have such incredibly talented friends and collaborators in my corner.

The final form of this book was guided by the sensitive and thoughtful suggestions of Helen Smith, Victoria Coulson, JT Welsch, and Michael White.

Numerous friends, colleagues, and mentors sustained me with constructive criticism and conversation at various stages of the project, especially Gillian Russell, Claire Chambers, Ella Barker, Bryony Aitchison, Alix Beeston, Cadence Kinsey, Abram Foley, and the members of the Essayisms reading group. I could not have done without Helen Barrett's incredible administrative support in the collection's final stages.

Writing and editing this book in the first of year of the pandemic made for a strange experience. My family, in various and loving ways, made the path easier, even from the other side of the world. Tamsin and Tom are friends for life—and make that life infinitely more entertaining.

Lastly, this book is ultimately one about looking together. It was finished during a time in which many of us couldn't, for many reasons, travel to galleries and museums, or wile away an afternoon in the company of art. I was struck that when searching for an escape from the news I wanted shelter from its paranoia but not to be shielded from its difficulty; these essays achieve both by offering aesthetic comradery, what John Berger called *hospitality*.

When life allows us those luxuries again, there is no one else with whom I would rather lose myself in art than you, Sam. Thank you.

Introduction The Art Essay

ALEXANDRA KINGSTON-REESE

In my study there hangs an artwork that I first saw in 2009. I was interning as an invigilator at a private art gallery owned by a couple who seemed to have impeccable taste. There was no kitsch in sight and the building itself was beautifully secluded, all wood and concrete. It was pitched on the side of a hill and surrounded on most sides by lines of trees. You wouldn't think it would be the perfect structure for the display of art, but from the inside the hard, opaque exteriors revealed hidden seams of glass. Light streamed in, no matter the weather outside. I would like to say my role in all of this carried with it an equal weight of aesthetic importance but in truth, the job sounded more impressive than it actually was. It seemed like the perfect opportunity to create the life I saw for myself—who wouldn't want to spend hours alone with works of art, gradually cultivating an aesthetically-tuned life of the mind?—but mostly I was there to dissuade drunk students and well-meaning members of the public from touching the art. Realizing I was a glorified bouncer was one of my first real lessons about the art world's banalities.

The works that hung on the walls that summer were by Marian Maguire, a lithographer who put modern artists and poets into conversation with classical subjects. I had excelled in my job interview, explaining with youthful enthusiasm how I had been studying art history and was fascinated most by printmaking (Albrecht Dürer's etchings in particular, which were somehow housed in the national museum down the road on the other side of the world from where they had been made), and how inspiring I found the idea of taking care of art, even in the most minimal fashion. I would be assiduous in my duties. That first week I was, walking a couple of circuits around the gallery, dutifully stopping for a brief pause in front of each work. But mostly, as the gallery turned out to be emptier than expected, I spent those long afternoons reading, drinking in the space's perennial Sunday feeling. Long slants of sunlight, dappled by the trees outside, stretched across the wooden floors marking the hours passing by. From time to time, I would glance up from the page to a figure in one of the prints, his arms lifted in dramatic posture and mouth open as if poised to speak. The whole scene is taut with anticipation. Only later did I realize that, of course, I had intentionally squandered time I would never get back, counting it down, trying to fill it. A gallery is a space of observation and, if you're lucky, the best ones direct your eye with casual architectural tricks. This one, with its floor-to-ceiling windows, was in more ways than most a space of intent looking—and I was looking away. I was trying to make time languish by resisting everything the space was designed to do.

Now, in front of me, through no lack of luck, there hangs this same print. And now, I glance at it every day from my desk. I rest my eyes on it compulsively—sometimes deliberately to look away from the screen, sometimes involuntarily in distraction or in thought. Sometimes on the figures' vacant eyes, sometimes on the hands, sometimes on the leaves above, wondering why there is no suggestion of a breeze. Though I have never stared at it for long periods of time, over the years these glances, I think, must have accumulated to several days of attention. To be sure, the glance is a kind of attention that brings all kinds of hazards. Inaccuracy, partiality, even laziness, are produced by a glance. Details are not quite lost because they are never apprehended in the first place. The glance is the mode of the impression, glancing off or leaving slight ripples in the eye. Its character leaves no room for growth or education; it glides across, finds the next surface to land on, and is gone.

But far from being entirely partial, the glance can equally lead to what Virginia Woolf called the quality of being "all eye." Writing about the painter Walter Sickert in the mid-1930s, in an episode staged as an imaginary dinner conversation, Woolf

> became completely and solely an insect—all eye. I flew from colour to colour, from red to blue, from yellow to green. Colours went spirally through my body lighting a flare as if a rocket fell through the night and lit up greens and browns, grass and trees, and there in the grass a white bird. Colour warmed, thrilled, chafed, burnt, soothed, fed and finally exhausted me. For though the life of colour is a glorious life it is a short one. Soon the eye can hold no more; it shuts itself in sleep, and if the man

who looks for cactuses had come by he would only have seen a shrivelled air-ball on a red plush chair.[1]

The spiraling motion of the prose leads us from one extreme to another, from a comfortable warmth to exhaustion, in no time at all. An utter depletion—all through the glance. Elsewhere Woolf wrote that "painting and writing have much to tell each other," and in diary entries from 1940 she often noted a desire to write a historical survey on literature for artists, in which she would attend to "the connection between seeing & writing," what she called "a twin gift."[2] This never-to-exist volume, which she had titled *Reading at Random*, would follow two earlier volumes of literary criticism called *The Common Reader* (1925 and 1932) that privileged the eclectic, individualized reading of the non-specialist. I like to think of *Reading at Random* as the "glance" in literary form, a visual conversation, where its vulnerability to amateurism is also precisely its gift.

■

This collection of essays offers up the same gesture. The art essay is born out of a glance—fragmentary, ephemeral, a slice of experience. And in this act of looking aslant, looking nimbly, the art essay is at once not about the art and all about the art—the glance at the piece of art evolves into a meditation on something else entirely. The glance is also an outstretching of arms to the reader with an invitation to finish the conversation. All good art writing works as communion. Between object and viewer, this is a process nothing less than alchemical, familiar, personal. When readers enter the fray, we are folded in, eavesdropping on intimate conversation, where the viewer and object work together to uncover some mutual understanding.

Art draws us in for different reasons, moves us strangely with our moods, our needs, our inspirations, and dilemmas. Although (or, perhaps, because) aesthetic experience is believed to actively defeat our ability to express feeling and thought—to render us tongue-tied—writers seem to be drawn to art more urgently than most. The forms of art have always been in a tense dance of perfection, purity, and status. One version of the history of the arts would turn this obsessive, competitive story into a romance. It would tell of writers' passionate relationship with the visual arts: the cautious courting, the heady early days, the time spent in each other's pockets, the fractious incompatibilities, the overdramatic denouncements, the eventual swearing off, the years of self-discovery, and a tender reembrace. As Lynette Yiadom-Boakye, the subject of Zadie Smith's essay in this collection, reflects: "I write about the things I can't paint and paint the things I can't write about."

The art essay confronts this formal incommensurability head on with renewed intensity. While we can find its roots in the work of Woolf, the art essay seems to be a peculiarly recently formed genre. For as long as there have been novels, there have been those peopled with artists, wannabe artists, and preening bohemians. The art novel laid some of the groundwork for the novelist's turn to art criticism. In George Eliot's *Middlemarch* (1871), meditative scenes on painting are almost essayistic. Consider Will Ladislaw on the superiority of literature to art: "Language gives a fuller image, which is all the better for being vague. After all, the true seeing is within; and painting stares at you with insistent imperfection." Contemporary versions of the art novel dip into essayistic modes as well, refracting a somewhat old-fashioned combination of subjects—art, beauty, aesthetic experience—through new lenses of ethics, politics, accessibility and inclusion, translation and multilingualism. In many instances—where a writer has written both—the art novel precedes the essay, perhaps offering a safer territory for aesthetic exploration. But increasingly, as the art essay becomes an established genre, the essay is the place where these things get worked out *for* the novel, as the essay as a form becomes the "bread and butter" of the working writer. This second line of conversation, this time between literary forms, reveals a second dilemma: the place where the writer is most forcibly aligned with the market even as they are trying to think about the unquantifiable value of aesthetics.

On art and sexuality, painting, photography, and women and art, art essays began to emerge as one-off pieces in literary magazines, as regular columns, as collections of essays around the end of the first decade of this century. Often, as if acting as a palette cleanser, they appeared in-between novels, when the emotional exertion of writing in one form was too great to do it all over again. Like many great essays, this collection started with a list, and the longer it got, the more this appeared to me as a distinct genre flourishing with divergent styles and subjects. From there, very quickly, I dreamt up a book in which the best examples of the genre could all be found together. This collection brings together and defines a style of essay that takes art both as its obsessive subject and as its formal foundation. Akin to what Michel Foucault says about form—it is "both instrument and object of research"—the art essay is an essay at once about, and aspiring towards being, art.[3]

Over the summer of 2019, when work on this book began in earnest, I built a wish list of essays by contemporary writers, many of them prize-winners, most of them novelists, some of whom I had written about before, others whose work I teach, and all whom I have long admired. I wanted this to be an energetic, unapologetic collection that shows the significant cultural impact of the art essay, but that tries to avoid its pitfalls. In their idiosyncrasy, art essays risk becoming beholden to the cultural objects they obsess over. "If the essay declines to begin by deriving cultural works from something underlying them," Theodor Adorno warned, "it embroils itself all too eagerly in the culture enterprise promoting the prominence, success, and prestige of marketable products."[4] While this is true of any essay, art essays are particularly distinguishable by their insider-ness, complicit in reinforcing cultural systems of prestige. The cultural power of the art essay is in part a product of editorial commissions: many art essays are devised by and for literary magazines (*Frieze*, *Harper's*, *New York Magazine*, *New York Review of Books*, and *Paris Review*). Too often art essays reexamine the same artists over and over again, and in turn are read by the same readers.

It was my priority that the essays here instead represent a wide spectrum of experience and attention, both in who is looking and what is being looked at. I have focused on essays from this century, and those that feature contemporary art, art by women, and art by neglected artists. There are essays on Picasso and Duchamp, but also on Leonora Carrington, Sonia Delaunay, Dawoud Bey, Omer Fast, Lynette Yiadom-Boakye, Dayanita Singh, and Elka Krajewska; there are essays on damaged art, photography, community art, and video installation, as well as on painting. These essays are about people and places, from Madrid and Mexico City, to the neighborhoods of Los Angeles and streets of Malaysia and New Delhi. Through the richness of its description, we can see the art essay as a songbook of contemporary viewership: here are portraits that remind us of our ethical duty; here is a mother's love; here are paintings of men and women bathed in yellows, reds, and blues.

■

Ever since Montaigne called his book of meditations *Essais* in 1580, the essay has been understood as a form that attempts, tests, and tries out ideas; from its etymological root upwards, it is a form, or else a form in "search for form" (William Gass), or "not a form" at all (Michael Hamburger). It is "thought itself in orbit" (Elizabeth Hardwick); "the mind in the marvels and miseries of its makings, in the *work* of the imagination" (Gass, again); "the equivalent of a mind in rumination" (John D'Agata); "a walk, an excursion, not a business trip" (Hamburger again). Even Virginia Woolf, when attempting to describe the essay, wound herself up to a beautifully ambivalent conclusion. The essay, she writes, "makes us suspect that the art of writing has for backbone some fierce attachment to an idea. It is on the back of an idea, something believed in with conviction or seen with precision and thus compelling words to its shape."[5] Knowing what we know about the essay, it is easy to understand why Woolf wedges herself into such an equivocal position. We can even forgive her for her vague aphorisms—she is writing an essay after all and this vague about-ism is endemic to essay form, always *on*, *about*; evasive.

As a form for ideas, then, the essay is naturally rooted in the tradition of criticism. It is not just a form that allows novelists to escape form, it offers a site to stake a claim *on* form; to dip their toes into the debate; to contribute to their own culture of reading. As Thomas Karshan and Kathryn Murphy describe in their recent volume *On Essays* (2020), "the spirit of the essay . . . is miscellaneous and anti-systematic"; it is, in Adorno's phrase, "methodically unmethodical."[6] Trying to pin down a genre so indeterminate, so equivocal, so ambivalent, Karshan continues, has been the occupation of the form itself, as essays have always "understood themselves evasively, preferring to define themselves by what they are not."[7]

This is all to say that while such conditions make for art, the essay has had a fraught history, often maligned as neither criticism nor literature. This ambivalence is due in part to the waning status of the essay in the middle of the twentieth century. The essay was all but put in cold storage, as other journalistic forms proved more versatile and profitable.[8] But the essay style could still be seen in new genres like the New Journalism coined by Tom Wolfe in 1973, which saw journalists place themselves directly in the action of their work, recalling the essayist's persona. The artificial divide between the two categories—journalism and essay—plagued the best-known postwar American cultural critics: Mary McCarthy, Susan Sontag, James Baldwin, and Joan Didion. Perhaps it has something to do with what we think essays are for. Looking at the essays of the writers I mention here, as long as their essays were written professionally to meet the unglamorous demands of making a living, they were classified as journalism. Once their status and financial stability was lifted by success with fiction, their critical writing was reclassified as essays. Even if the essay wasn't literature itself, it was tied to other established, and easily classifiable, forms.

This was Woolf's claim: "there is no room for the impurities of literature in an essay." What these impurities are for Woolf, we can only guess, but she nevertheless insisted that "the essay must be pure—pure like water or pure like wine, but pure from dullness, deadness, and deposits of extraneous matter."[9] There are some problems with this characterization. Firstly, the essay as *pure* form—a purity New Journalism also carried off in spirit—has encouraged a particularly masculine literary history of the essay as aesthetically taut and strangely unyielding. Secondly, the perfection or purity that Woolf is referring to lies paradoxically in the form's imperfections. (Isn't the essay *all* "extraneous matter"? Brian Dillon asks.[10]) The essay is self-contained, neat, and self-resolving precisely because these writers do not have to respond to bigger issues—they can avoid grappling with the politics of their subjects, end in the middle of discussion, rely on parataxis, accumulation of description, and, in lieu of conclusion, end with what Georges Perec called "the art of enumeration," an "etc."

But as much as Woolf was concerned about muddling of essay form with the impurities of literature, the art essay doesn't impugn the literary at all. It wears its learning on its sleeve, but also decorates itself; its stylistic appeal is that it dwells in joyous description with particular virtuosity. Some live elliptically in the fragment; in catalogue; as a list; in a cabinet of curiosities, a *Wunderkammer*. Some employ slow and loving looking, others glance at speed. Then there are those that, on reading, make you feel like you've just got caught in a downpour.

■

The essays in this collection harness the peculiar language of sight. As a young Hilton Als recounted discovering when he was just starting out as an art historian, "to *see*, one must possess a language which directs the eyes to what is being perceived."[11] Learning this language is a lifelong occupation, something to be nurtured and tested. In this respect, it is not like any other kind of language; this language has no grammar, no dictionary. In her memoir about learning Italian, *In Other Words*, Jhumpa Lahiri wrote that "Every language belongs to a specific place. It can migrate, it can spread. But usually it's tied to a geographical territory, a country."[12] The language of seeing doesn't belong to a place, though perhaps it finds a home in the art essay, a genre that blends two complementary styles of viewership. A discipline of seeing, of critical love.

In the mid-nineteenth century, John Ruskin suggested that the poet's knowledge of the world was commensurate with a painter's way of looking. The "difference between the mere botanist's knowledge of plants, and the great poet's or painter's knowledge of them," he wrote, is that "the one notes their distinctions for the sake of swelling his herbarium, the other, that he may render them vehicles of expression and emotion."[13] The botanist is happy to catalogue, name, and count, while the artist "considering each of its attributes as an element of expression ... seizes on its lines of grace or energy, rigidity or repose; notes the feebleness or the vigor, the serenity or tremulousness of its hues; observes its local habits, its love or fear of peculiar places, its nourishment or destruction by particular influences."

There is something of the artist in the essayist, too. Dillon describes essayistic meditation as an "exercise in deliberate attention" as "necessarily a lapse, a relaxing into a sort of supine and uncritical mode" that "demands a certain weakness or passivity."[14] It is important to note that Dillon is referring to *critical* weakness here, an intentional refusal of attending to art *in extremis*, adverse to the ableist machismo of critique that literary critics sought to overthrow in recent years in favor of modest forms of criticism. We see this modesty in many of the essayists in this collection who claim their dilettantish, amateurish love for art couldn't possibly count for expertise. Zadie Smith at one stage noted that "essays about one person's affective experience have, by their very nature, not a leg to stand on. . . . all they have is their freedom." Freedom—to look, feel, write—is nothing to be sniffed at; and *true* intellectual freedom has everything to admire.

With training in description, discursion, care, curiosity, and sentimentality, here we find the irreverent potential of the art essay. In this vein, we see Heidi Sopinka travel to Mexico City to find a death guide in Leonora Carrington; we see Geoff Dyer travel to New Delhi to discover what makes photographer Dayanita Singh's Dream Villa tick; we see Chris Kraus meditating on the artistic community in her local neighborhood in Los Angeles; we see Jhumpa Lahiri spending time in Simon Dinnerstein's studio, considering the ties that make families; we see Claire-Louise Bennett drawn to Dorothea Tanning, unable to sleep, "because of the hatred I felt towards anything I managed to write—a tenacious affliction which produced highly resourceful night phantoms. They kept me awake all night through with their inventive jibes and searing remonstrations. Look at how creative and fearless we are! And look at how dull and craven you have become!"[15]

Just as these writers each practice and make visible for us a different kind of gaze—whether it is close attention, persistently training the eye across a wide landscape, or a series of rapid glances—so too do the essays themselves yield to different kinds of reading. The reader who prefers to follow closely will discover a whole catalogue of different forms of attention, from the loving gaze to the cold eye. The reader who opts to glance quickly, darting here and there, might instead make connections between shared landmarks, motifs repeated or reimagined, that a closer view might obscure.

Rather than privileging one way of reading over the other, I have opted to arrange the essays in what may seem like the most cursory order—alphabetically, by last name. This arrangement serendipitously positions Chloe Aridjis at the beginning; following one of the most idiosyncratic styles of looking in the collection, Aridjis's essay is itself an alphabetical list, revealing the kind of unexpected connections that can come from apparently constrained ways of looking. The fact that Aridjis's subject is Leonora Carrington—a long-time family friend of the author—only emphasises the fact that formal distance does not preclude intimacy. Aridjis's essay embodies the art essay's capacity for closeness. And for those readers drawn to the idea of eavesdropping on intimate conversation, the "Thematic Guide to Approaching the Essays" gives readers several possible itineraries if they prefer to trace some of the threads of interest that connect these writers' gazes and voices. Of course, a quick glance at the names in the contents and a quiet moment spent sharing the company of one or two has its own rewards. But attending to art, as the essays in this collection show, results in an improved quality of attention: on language, grief, history, waiting, shopping, family, love, sleep, and being haunted. The essay is the perfect form for allowing one's will to become pliable through the simple act of observation, open to the search, to the banality of situation. The essays included here attach the greatest significance to the smallest of things, bringing attention itself to the highest altitudes and lowest depths.

These essays ask us to reimagine not only the aesthetic and cultural power of literary engagements with the experience of art, but the political power too—for in a world often devoid of subtlety and nuance, what could be more political than choosing to rest in slow, deep, sustained looking?

Notes

1. Virginia Woolf, *Walter Sickert: A Conversation* (London: Hogarth Press, 1934), https://www.gutenberg.ca/ebooks/woolfv-waltersickert/woolfv-waltersickert-00-e.html.
2. Woolf's "Notes for Reading at Random" were first published in 1979 in "'Anon' and 'The Reader': Virginia Woolf's Last Essays," ed. Brenda R. Silver, *Twentieth Century Literature*, Virginia Woolf Issue 25, no. 3/4 (Autumn–Winter 1979): 377.
3. Michel Foucault, *The Archaeology of Knowledge*, trans. A. M. Sheridan Smith (New York: Harper and Row, 1972), 9.
4. Theodor Adorno, "The Essay as Form," *Notes to Literature I*, trans. Shierry Weber Nicholsen (New York: Columbia University Press, 1991), 5.
5. Virginia Woolf, "The Modern Essay," in *Selected Essays*, ed. David Bradshaw (Oxford: Oxford University Press, 2008), 21.
6. Thomas Karshan and Kathryn Murphy, "Introduction: On the difficulty of introducing a work of this kind," in *On Essays: Montaigne to the Present*, ed. Thomas Karshan and Kathryn Murphy (Oxford: Oxford University Press, 2020); Adorno, "The Essay as Form," 13.

7. Thomas Karshan, "What is an Essay? Thirteen Answers from Virginia Woolf," in *On Essays: Montaigne to the Present*, ed. Thomas Karshan and Kathryn Murphy (Oxford: Oxford University Press, 2020).
8. For more on this see Robert Atwan, "Notes towards the Definition of the Essay," in *Essayists on the Essay: Montaigne to Our Time*, ed. Ned Stuckey-French and Carl H. Klaus (Iowa City: University of Iowa Press, 2012).
9. Woolf, "The Modern Essay," 14.
10. Brian Dillon, *Essayism: On Form, Feeling, and Nonfiction* (New York: New York Review of Books, 2017), 17.
11. Hilton Als, "The First Step of Becoming an Art Historian," *Black American Literature Forum*, Contemporary Black Visual Artists Issue 19, no. 1 (Spring 1985): 28.
12. Jhumpa Lahiri, *In Other Words*, trans. Ann Goldstein (London: Bloomsbury, 2016), 19.
13. John Ruskin, *Modern Painters* (New York: John Wiley, 1848), xxxiv.
14. Dillon, *Essayism*, 144.
15. Claire-Louise Bennett, *Fish Out of Water* (Milan: Juxta Press, 2019).

Thematic Guide to Approaching the Essays

If you would prefer not to read the essays in arbitrary sequence, the following thematic guide offers you alternative routes through the collection.

Friendship: The Romantics, the Bloomsbury group, the New York School: writers and artists tend to move in the same circles, courting semi-intimate friendships and professional collaborations. As Tash Aw noted about Ian Teh: "when we'd already become friends, we joked about how people from similar backgrounds have a habit of making connections with each other thousands of miles from home, but that first day, it seemed entirely natural that we should meet; our crossing paths didn't feel coincidental." To read for friendship, start with Chloe Aridjis on Leonora Carrington, follow with Heidi Sopinka on Leonora Carrington, Chris Kraus on Los Angeles's art ecosystem, Jhumpa Lahiri on Simon Dinnerstein, and finish with Aw on Teh.

Motherhood: Art writing is haunted by myths about femininity and motherhood. The essays in this collection don't care for these stereotypes, however. For Ali Smith, the combination of being an artist and a mother is "an act of love," but as Heidi Sopinka notes, it is also an act of death: "Four years earlier and six weeks too soon, I'd given birth to a baby. You might say my death drive, as Freud calls it, had made itself known." Start with Smith's essay, follow with Sopinka's and end with Jhumpa Lahiri on Simon Dinnerstein.

Place: Often the place in which we encounter art is as important as the direct experience itself. Ben Lerner has called this the epiphenomena of aesthetic experience, which is "less concerned with detailing the object than the total environment in which the artistic encounter takes place." While he notes that it is "prose fiction [that] can allow you to offer a robust description of all the epiphenomena and contingencies involved in a particular character's encounter with a particular work: it allows you to place that encounter in a character's life, time, day, describing not only a quality of light in a gallery, but what the character has read or eaten or smoked, what was on his or her mind on that morning or evening, what protest they passed on the way to the museum, etc." here we see how the essay form allows this quality of attention. Start with Tash Aw in Malaysia, catch a train to Geoff Dyer in India, fly to Chris Kraus in Los Angeles, but join Claire-Louise Bennett in Madrid on a stopover, and drive down the coast to Heidi Sopinka in Mexico City.

Portraits: The portrait is an exemplar of our ethical duty to the other, even if it might be imaginary. "The face speaks to me, and thereby invites me to a relation," as the philosopher Emmanuel Lévinas puts it; "the face means identity, truth, feeling, beauty, authenticity, humanity," as Namwali Serpell writes. Teju Cole, when writing about Dawoud Bey, is attuned to the flawed use of photography for physiognomy; begin with this essay and follow with Tash Aw on Ian Teh, and Zadie Smith on Lynette Yiadom-Boakye. Attend to self-portraits next.

Self-portraits: Writing essays and looking at art both involve self-reflection, and yet can also involve extricating art from biography. As Hanya Yanagihara writes about David Wojnarowicz's self-portraits, his art "swept up the entirety of who the artist was and what he had experienced—and had seen and felt—into a single image and spat it back out at the viewer; there is a shimmering present-tenseness to it." The essayist always occupies a shimmering, *simmering* persona, too, Virginia Woolf argued: "Never to be yourself and yet always—that is the problem." Start with Yanagihara on Wojnarowicz, Ali Smith on Sonia Delaunay, Sheila Heti on Sara Cwynar, followed by Claire-Louise Bennett on Dorothea Tanning, and end with Jhumpa Lahiri on Simon Dinnerstein and his family.

Translation: Translation speaks to more than the linguistic gap between seeing and writing. I am drawn most to the art essay by writers who are used to moving between languages—Bengali, Yoruba, French, Italian, English—because this quality is distinctive to aesthetic experience, too. Translating the untranslatable—whether a foreign word, or an experience into artistic form—constitutes "a kind of slowing down of language," where writers are required to be careful, deliberate, and attentive to language as a tool that is both communicative and aesthetic. Even John Berger's famous *Ways of Seeing* (1972), to which many of the essayists in this collection are aesthetically in debt, begins with this untranslatability: "the relation between what we see and what we know is never settled. Each evening we see the sun set. We know that the earth is turning away from it. Yet the knowledge, the explanation, never quite fits the sight." Start with Jhumpa Lahiri, Teju Cole, Heidi Sopinka, and Geoff Dyer.

Women: Contemporary art essays perform recuperative feminist projects. As Leonora Carrington herself remarked about women, "You have to own your soul, as far as it's possible to own your soul—or for it to own you. But to give it over to some half-assed male? I wouldn't recommend it." Start with Ali Smith on Sonia Delaunay, Claire-Louise Bennett on Dorothea Tanning, Sheila Heti on Sara Cwynar, and end with Chloe Aridjis's and Heidi Sopinka's essays on Carrington.

The collection is also traversable via form:

Painting: Ali Smith on Sonia Delaunay, Claire-Louise Bennett on Dorothea Tanning, Jhumpa Lahiri on Simon Dinnerstein, Hanya Yanagihara on David Wojnarowicz, Zadie Smith on Lynette Yiadom-Boakye.

Photography: Tash Aw on Ian Teh, Teju Cole on Dawoud Bey, Geoff Dyer on Dayanita Singh.

Video Art: Start with Katie Kitamura on Omer Fast: "The feeling I had, the first time I saw *Nostalgia*, was that Omer Fast was evidently one of the best fiction writers working today." End with Sheila Heti on Sara Cwynar (whose "films are delicious").

Essays

Chloe Aridjis

Chloe Aridjis is a London-based Mexican novelist and essayist, the author of *Book of Clouds* (2009), *Asunder* (2013), and *Sea Monsters* (2019), as well as several essays for *Frieze Magazine*. In 2015, Aridjis co-curated with Francesco Manacorda the Tate retrospective of Leonora Carrington, the surrealist artist at the center of this essay. In 2018, Aridjis starred in *Female Human Animal*, a film by Josh Appignanesi, which centers on this exhibition. Playing a character version of herself, the film is infected with Carrington's surrealism and disenchantment with modern life. Aridjis was a close friend of Carrington before the latter's death in 2011, noting in one piece for *Frieze* how, when taking photographs of the artist in her home in Mexico City, her space seemed under Carrington's spell: "[I was] struck by the procession of instruments hanging behind where Leonora was seated. Their shadows—evoking claws, shovels, tridents, horned creatures—were imbued with a *Fantasia* sorcerer's potential, and I half expected them to come alive and start marching around." This is just one of three critical pieces Aridjis has written on Carrington; the list essay in this collection is another. List essays are the ultimate essay form (essays that utilize the list are essays about essays), as they require real work to close them in finality. Aridjis's alphabet essay short-circuits this danger of the list never being done, foreclosing the necessary "etc" of tailing off by tricking us into thinking the list is complete through a literal exhaustion of language. Writing an alphabet version for Carrington's 100th birthday makes sense; the symmetry of one hundred and the finality of the alphabet make a list that is itself necessarily finite, but not hierarchical; instead, it is additive, conjunctive, paratactic.

A Leonora Carrington A to Z

Leonora Carrington would have turned 100 today. I met her in Mexico City in the early 1990s, through our family doctor, and we embarked on a friendship of nearly twenty years. Most Sunday afternoons, my parents, my sister and I would visit her at home in the Colonia Roma, arriving at five and staying until after dusk. I often wrote down my impressions, and her words verbatim, as soon as I got home.

■

Ambidextrous: Leonora could write and paint with both hands at once, forwards and backwards. "Yes, I'm ambidextrous, like madmen," she once said.

Bullfighting: "Horrific. It's a disgusting, shameful demonstration of human stupidity and cruelty. Horrible. I was once put out at a bullfight. I got up and clapped when the bull jumped over the thing and chased all the attendants around, and I just clapped and clapped, and they put me out."

Cats: The last cats Leonora owned were Ramona and Monsieur, two green-eyed Siamese who followed her around the house. She wanted a dog too but worried the cats would stop speaking to her.

Devils: "I think there are very dangerous devils, and I think there are interesting devils, and I think there are very stupid devils, I think there are probably intelligent ones, and angels and anything that has been invented. Hundreds, thousands of them, all over the place.... Well, I use the word *invented* when I mean seen. I don't know what *invented* means, really, do you?"

England: Leonora would express nostalgia for England but at the same time no desire to return. She missed the trees and the architecture rather than the people, since most of those she knew had died, and the eventful moments of her life had taken place abroad.

Filters: Until her final days, Leonora smoked. Her choice of cigarette varied but she always attached them to short plastic filters, which she would clean and reuse.

Gray: More than anything, Leonora wore gray. Baggy gray trousers, long gray sweaters, gray shawls, gray turtlenecks, gray lace-up shoes. Occasionally she'd bring in a bit of purple but my memory of her is distinctly in monochrome.

Haunting: Leonora would sometimes mention a middle-aged woman in pink who'd appear in different rooms. A few friends claimed to see the ghost too, standing behind her. She was never scared, however; in previous times, her home had been a printing house, "which is not a very sinister thing."

Imagination: "Nothing is created by the imagination. Imagination is a very mysterious force which we know very little about. We don't know if it creates anything.... I think that things occur, like for instance somebody one time must have invented a cup, because it was easier than putting your face into a river and lapping up the water."

James, Edward: Englishman in Mexico, patron of the Surrealists; Leonora was fond of him, despite saying he lacked respect for his friends and would wash his hands with her shampoo.

Kabbalah: The book Leonora would mention most often, important to her throughout her lifetime.

Lapland: Often when we'd ask Leonora what place she would most like to visit, she would reply: "Lapland." She loved reindeer and wished the Lapps would stop eating them.

Manipulation: She said manipulation is what makes "the great cosmic yoghurt."

Nagas: Some of Leonora's favorite mythical creatures, from Indian mythology, which featured in her paintings and sculptures.

Orange Pekoe: Leonora would often ask me to bring her a tin of tea from England, especially Orange Pekoe. She also loved PG Tips, "bog standard English tea," and said she much preferred it to fancy teas. Whatever I brought her she would keep under lock and key so that no one else could use it. "Cacher la boîte de PG Tips."

Painting: "I rarely paint images from dreams. Images occur just like that. They occur from something that is further away from my consciousness, I think. But any painter would tell you that."

"**Q**uel désir d'extravagance!" André Breton's words on first seeing her paintings, in Paris, when Leonora was twenty.

Roma: Colonia Roma was the neighborhood of Mexico City she lived in from the 1940s; over the decades, it underwent an enormous transformation. Across the street lay the debris of a collapsed building, a victim of the 1985 earthquake, which housed a growing community of cats and homeless people. Leonora called it "a garden of scorpions."

Spiritualism: Leonora could see through the hocus pocus of people who claimed to have supernatural powers. She once played a trick on a "very serious ex-Nazi with a thick German accent" who held a séance. She brought along one of her sons and before the session they attached a small instrument to the bottom of the table. It made metallic noises whenever it was pulled by a string. Everyone sat down. After a while, Leonora began to grow bored. She or her son pulled the string. Noises were heard coming from beneath the table. "I think there's something there," Leonora said. "Who are you?" the ex-Nazi asked. "I think it's a horse," Leonora replied. The man stood up and tipped the table over to reveal the hidden instrument. He was livid, and never spoke to Leonora again.

Time: "I don't need to kill time. It's killing me." (When asked whether she played chess, she said she was uninterested in board games, and would rather draw.)

University of contraception: Leonora would often complain there were too many people in the world and wished they would establish such a university.

Varo, Remedios: Feline-faced Spanish painter, one of Leonora's closest female friends, with whom she shared a love of cats.

Weisz, Emerico, also known as Chiki: Hungarian photographer to whom Leonora was married for over fifty years, largely in silence.

Xanax (Tafil in Mexico): Leonora would take half a tablet every night for sleep and anxiety. "The darkness" would set in by late afternoon, she said.

Yeti: Leonora's last pet (after Ramona and Monsieur: see **C**ats), a small, white, hyperactive Maltese.

Zoology: Leonora adored animals, mythical and real. "I draw completely from my mind. Well, I don't know if it's my mind.... But if I'm drawing an animal like a cat, I'd like to draw it from life."

Tash Aw

Tash Aw is a London-based novelist and essayist. Raised in Malaysia, he is the author of four novels: *The Harmony Silk Factory* (2005), *Map of the Invisible World* (2009), *Five Star Billionaire* (2013), and *We, The Survivors* (2019), all of which revolve around questions of Malaysian identity, migration, and the long tail of history. Since 2014, he has been a regular contributor of reviews and op-eds to the *New York Times*, and he has written essays on everything from badminton players for the *Guardian* and Malaysian import policies for *Granta*, to the poetics of broken bridges for the *Fabulist*. Like his subject in this essay on Malaysian photographer Ian Teh, Aw often reflects on his own distanced connection to his two homes, Britain and Malaysia. Although he believes that "at its best," writing "changes the way one sees the world and oneself; it asks questions, even if it can't provide the answers," he also notes that "at its banal worst, of course it changes nothing." Far from banal, his essay on Teh pays precise attention to the formal mastery of the photographs, even as Aw traces the way the photographs (like his ideal essay) change his own view of the world and himself, charting the "glorious feeling of disorientedness" and "recognition of . . . foreignness" that the photographs provoke.

You Need to Look Away

Visions of Contemporary Malaysia

Comel is the daughter of a mamasan, a woman who runs one of several local brothels. Sometimes, in the afternoons, when her husband is out, Comel also turns the occasional trick, but otherwise she's like any other twenty-one-year-old in the area, lively, chatty, obsessed by her smartphone. She is a sex worker who is not really a sex worker, hovering between two worlds.

Both mother and daughter are married to Indonesians, one a sailor, the other a migrant worker. At the end of the month, on pay day, they can see the dock workers queuing up at the ATM on the other side of the highway, waiting to draw out enough money to spend the evening with a girl. Here in the northern stretch of Port Klang, Malaysia's busiest port, nightlife is sparse, and what there is feels gritty and distinctly unglamorous, a different world from the sophisticated Western-style bars and restaurants of the capital, Kuala Lumpur, only an hour's drive away. The country's gateway to the sea, Port Klang and the surrounding coastline seem to be disconnected from the rest of Selangor, the richest and most populous state in Malaysia, as if all the trade and industry that flows through its docks has decided to settle elsewhere, bypassing the coastline altogether.

The women live in an area of dilapidated shop houses hemmed in by a massive new elevated highway that separates them from the rest of North Port. This new road casts a shadow on the area where Comel and her friends live, the houses becoming shabbier with each passing year. Over time, some have collapsed entirely, leaving ghostly spaces in the rows of once-fine shophouses; others now have Ficus trees sprouting from their masonry, their roots further destroying the fabric of these buildings. As for the fabric of the lives that occupy this area, there is a sense, too, that they are caught in a sort of stasis, cut off from the hubris of economic development elsewhere in the port, and indeed in the steadily modernizing country beyond. Yet Comel and her friends live with a sort of optimism that belongs to the narrative of "1Malaysia," the government's campaign to promote national

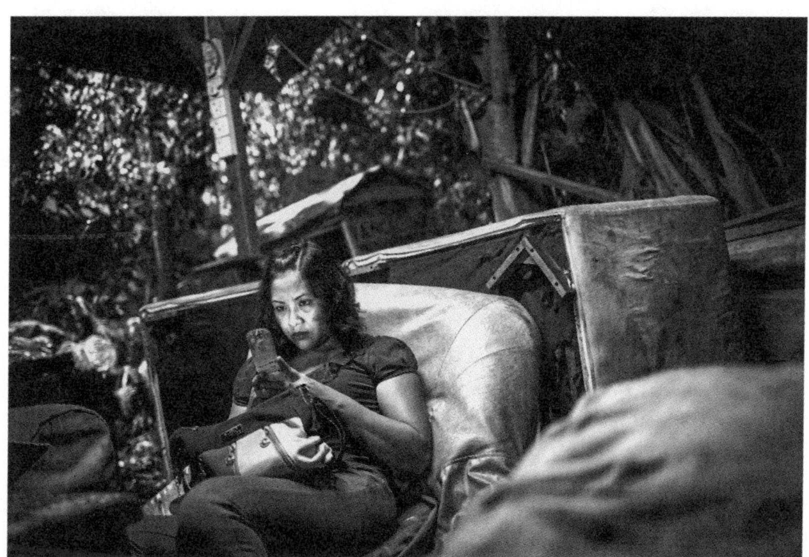

Ian Teh, "A First-Generation Migrant from Indonesia Married to a Local, Port Klang." © Ian Teh. Courtesy of the artist.

togetherness and industry: they are part of the idea of a progressive, can-do country riding the swell of the material transformations taking place in Asia in the 21st century. Like so much else in photographer Ian Teh's work, she occupies that space in between two worlds, two conflicting realities. She both is and isn't what she appears to be, nor—crucially—what she wants to be.

Abstract beauty collides with the hard-edged reality of contemporary Asia in Ian Teh's photographs, producing an effect that is at once mesmerizing and disconcerting. If his subject is the world of the unseen—the people and landscapes that are everywhere, but strikingly unnoticed—then his images, too, draw the viewer into that nebulous space between admiration and revulsion, though there is barely a difference between them. In his universe, the two are linked; so, too, the wondrous and the banal, the magical and the horribly real. Sometimes it is difficult even to know what you are looking at. Every time you venture into one emotional space, his work calls you back into another.

He and I first met in London in 2011, when he was taking my portrait for an Olympics photography exhibition the following year. London-based photographers had been asked to photograph someone from their country of origin, and, through a series of chance connections involving mutual friends from Beijing, we met and Ian asked me to sit for a portrait. Much later, when we'd already become friends, we joked about how people from similar backgrounds have a habit of making connections with each other thousands of miles from home, but that first day, it seemed entirely natural that we should meet; our crossing paths didn't feel coincidental. We were born in the same year and moved to Britain in our teens—he at thirteen, with his mother, I five years later to attend university; we grew up in ethnic-Chinese families in Malaysia, the first of the new middle-class, neither rich nor poor, one generation away from poverty, yet brought up to believe in the possibilities of education and employment in a rapidly industrializing country. Our families remained largely in Malaysia, leaving us anchored in two vastly different countries and cultures—a cultural background that shaped our shared view of the world.

Throughout the three sittings for the portrait, we talked about how growing up as ethnic-Chinese in a Muslim-majority country meant being constantly aware of our immigrant roots, of having some distant connection with peoples and cultures seemingly far removed from our home. We were insiders who were also, in a small but profound sense, outsiders. And, by choosing to live in Britain, we have, in a way, turned ourselves into double immigrants. Perhaps this is why in my novels and his photography we're both preoccupied with outsiders—not just people who are marginalized by poverty or discrimination or lack of opportunity, but those who struggle to find their place in the world; people who, like Comel, fall into the cracks between the neatly defined categories that life lays down for us.

Take his large-format landscapes *Traces*. When the series was shown at the Flowers East Gallery in Shoreditch, London, I first saw ravishing images of snowy landscapes in the industrial heartland of northern China. Shimmering white peaks gracefully scarred by meandering rivers; frosted poplars standing against fields of snow. Once the initial frisson of beauty wore off, though, I realized they're not mountains of earth and stone, but giant piles of industrial waste; the rivers not torrents of melted snow, but streams of slag, run-off from the steel and other factories nearby; toxic waste shines whiter than snow, and pollution, not frost, settles on the trees. The eye takes in one thing, the intellect another. Yet Ian is not making a judgment here. There are no tiny clues that push you to appreciate the images as Beautiful Art or social commentary. Beauty is deceptive, the photographs say, but by indulging in it, are we also somehow tacitly participating in the destruction of our landscape? Or, conversely, having destroyed what we have? Do we now contemplate that loss and see a strange, haunting beauty?

When I left the gallery that day I was confused by the way the photographs had restructured my notions of beauty. The humanity of Ian's work, I remember thinking, lies in its openness, its ability to share the wondrous and terrifying possibilities of the way Asia is developing.

In *Confluence*, his sweeping yet sometimes chokingly personal portrait of Comel's Selangor coastline, he allies powerful social commentary with details that can seem, to me, suffused with melancholy. In an exhibition that opened last week in Kuala Lumpur's Publika, objects and beings usually overlooked take center stage. A herd of cows stares mournfully at the camera; a sow rears out of its pen on a pig farm; a hand-scrawled notice in bad Malay exhorts people not to litter or play loud music; a kitsch framed picture of a bucolic European landscape hangs marooned on a bare wall's flaking plaster. People come and go in these images, flitting in and out of the frame, almost as if they don't want to be there. Their expressions are distant, distracted: they are elsewhere, their thoughts occupying a different terrain.

Malaysia is a country built on migration—from the descendants of Arab sea traders who first arrived in the twelfth century, to the waves of indentured laborers from India and China in the nineteenth century, to the historic links with Sumatra and Java. Malaysia's culture is inextricably tied to the evolving histories of its neighbors, tied to a narrative of journeys. So it's unsurprising that much of *Confluence* focuses on the migrant workers who are a growing part of daily life in most parts of the country, and who are particularly pronounced along this stretch of the west coast—recent immigrants from Indonesia, Bangladesh and Burma, who reflect Malaysia's economic rise over the last thirty years, and its relative wealth in South East Asia. The unattached, almost absent nature of many of the subjects' gazes suggests a sense of dislocation, their presence immediately raising questions of belonging. Are they comfortable in their new surroundings? How do they see themselves—as temporary economic workers or as part of a new wave of immigrants? How is society stratifying into rich and poor in contemporary South East Asia? What is the gap between the privileged and the forgotten?

Workers stand in the midst of plantations, or while away time at the harbor as night falls. They have jobs, they are sending money home, they are working. But in Ian's images their expressions are tentative, caught between aggression and fear, neither defeated nor optimistic. And their stares become a statement of presence that invites us to enter their world.

His work has long had a sense of loss, but while the threat of a world on the brink of change looms large in *Traces*, here the feeling is more intimate, and more personal to Ian and me. A sequence of images charting a funeral recounts a real, physical passing, but even the living seem to have let go of something essential to their beings. Where, for example, are the wives, children, parents of these migrant workers? What have they given up to be here? And what of the physical structures, those magnificent old Chinese stuccoed shophouses, half-destroyed and on the brink of total collapse? Elsewhere, perfunctory modern apartment blocks stand ghostly and empty, as they often do in his portraits of contemporary Asian housing, as if they have given up the right to host life—as if they are all too aware of the passing on of things here in modern Malaysia. It's this giving up of something precious, the passing on of things—either voluntarily or forced by time or other circumstances—that I find moving, even troubling. Perhaps it's because of my own background, because of the anxiety that invariably accompanies moving from one culture to another, and that never really disappears. Perhaps it's because the study of migrant workers and others who have yet to nail down their positions in the world reminds me of what my ancestors must have been given up in order to start a new life.

■

One of the occasional treats I had as a child was a drive out to Carey Island for a Sunday lunch of chili crab in one of the many famous seafood restaurants that dotted the coastline south of Port Klang, the area that forms the subject of *Confluence*. The family would pile into our Ford Cortina and meander along roads that traced the broad sweeps of the muddy rivers that cut through Selangor and converge at this stretch of the coast, emptying into the Straits of Malacca. We'd cross little bridges over brackish inlets that smelled of rotting vegetation and brine. The restaurants were wooden shacks built on stilts over these inlets, and we would toss the empty crab shells over the sides of the wooden banisters into the water after picking the flesh from them. At low tide the waters would retreat to expose rusty oil drums and old boats mired in the mud; occasionally the waiters would empty entire dishes of crab shells and other food scraps to be carried away on high tide. Of those days I remember a glorious feeling of disorientedness—we were far enough away from the bustle of Petaling Jaya, the largest suburb in Selangor, where we lived, to feel that we were in the countryside, but not far enough to feel properly in the wilderness. Container ships dotted the horizon on their way to and from Port Klang; we could never tell if they were even moving.

I am connected to the landscape that Ian Teh portrays in *Confluence* by delicate threads of memory, but what draws me to it as an adult is a recognition of its foreignness—the way it is always present in the consciousness of Selangor dwellers yet rarely visited by them. We live a mere twenty or thirty miles from the coast, yet would much more readily drive the five hours to Penang, half the length of the west coast, just for the weekend. It is a place of trade and movement, of the meeting of land and sea, of freshwater and saltwater, a fluid mélange of cultures, yet it remains invisible to the affluent suburbs elsewhere in Selangor, home to the most affluent suburbs in the country.

Looking at Ian's images of the funeral, I remember my grandfather's similarly elaborate Chinese funeral in Perak. I remember the burning sun, the rituals, the sadness laced with boredom and fatigue, the long period of mourning afterwards. Above all, I remember the same bewilderment that I see on the faces of the mourners here. The funeral is a pig farmer's. We don't know what's going to happen to the farm, whether the children will take over or whether it will slip into ruin. Suddenly the pig that rears from its pen takes on a new anxiety. I remember staring at the empty chicken coop in the back of my grandfather's house in the days after his funeral. The chickens he reared for food became pets, well-fed hens that clucked and shat in a space under the air well close to the shophouse. When he died, the chickens were slaughtered to feed the dozens of friends and relatives who came to mourn. I knew they'd never be replaced.

Everywhere in Ian Teh's photographs I feel the vulnerability that permeates Roland Barthes's strange yet seminal little book on photography, *Camera Lucida*, and I understand, finally, all its statements that previously I found infuriatingly subjective. *In order to see a photograph well, you need to look away.* It seems clear to me now that what Barthes meant was that you have to delve into memory in order to understand what lies before you, but that the act of recalling risks casting doubt on the certainty of the image you are beholding. We can subject a photograph to any amount of objective artspeak we like, but ultimately we bring our own subjective understanding to each image. Barthes went in search of images of his dead mother, but none represented the person he knew or loved. In those photos he recognized his mother objectively, but couldn't feel her. She was familiar yet unknown. Ultimately he did find an image that represented her truly, as he remembered her. She was five years old in that picture, standing in a winter garden in 1898, a place and time he had never known. Suddenly: an onrush of memories. He cries. And then every photograph for him becomes a morbid memorial, an anticipation of "total, undialectical death," including his own.

I don't discern the shadow of death in Ian Teh's photographs, but rather a constant anticipation of the passing of things; and in this way his work throws light on the original title of Barthes's book: *La Chambre Claire*—the bright, light-filled room, the opposite of la chambre noire, the darkroom. Our real understanding of photographs lies away from the negatives and the printing and the labs, away from the objectivity that the camera lens and digital technology provide us; it lies in a space that we appreciate instinctively, a space that is tied to memory, to our own anxieties and aspirations. The best photography leads us to such spaces of illumination and lets us grapple with our vulnerabilities. The best photography is beyond beauty, even beyond meaning.

■

In four night scenes that revolve around the gritty reality of Comel's world, the derelict buildings and brothels are presented as a dreamscape, populated by people who don't seem quite attached to that land, who live a floating life despite the coarse demands of their everyday lives. Lit by eerie phantom colors, these photographs often seem more nightmarish than dreamy. Ultraviolet blue contrasted with glowing, hellish orange; overbright yellow, so luminous it seems to have been artificially cast by stage lights; tentative fluorescent lighting: there is all the shimmering terror of a nightmare in these photographs, where the people seem otherworldly, the physical structures illusory, leaving us uncertain of where we stand.

The empty space between two old stone shophouses suggests that a third was pulled down at some time in the past. Rubble on one side of the hollowed-out gap stretches into darkness. Objects lurk in the shadows—we can just about discern the outlines of a shed? The glint of an enormous blade? In the foreground, a transgender sex worker sits on a pile of rocks, waiting for clients. We can't see her features clearly but from a distance her face appears powdery white. With an eerie beauty, the photograph crystallizes our unconscious fears. It's a vision of what we think might happen when all life has departed, and what's left is consumed by forces more primeval and powerful and threatening than those which fill our domestic lives. It can't be real; it's something from our imagination and yet it is real. It exists a mere twenty miles from our pleasant suburbs.

A cheap, ancient Datsun stands outside a banal two-story house—both so innocuous they barely merit a second look, and the building hardly suggests a whorehouse. The rooms are lit by the cheap, blinding fluorescent tubes, but one room upstairs lies ominously dark. Who is in it? Yet outside, under a small tree, a woman and small child play in the balmy evening the way parents play with their children all over the world. We don't know which reality this scene belongs to. The image suggests "underworld" but it's also a commonplace neighborhood scene in this part of Malaysia. The shadow that looms ominously is a man, we think, but is he coming or going? Is he a father or a client, or perhaps both? In order to understand the photograph, we have to look elsewhere. We have to look at that man.

So, too, the two men hurrying down the arched walkway in front of the row of shophouses. On their left are lowered bamboo blinds; ahead of them at the end of their tunnel is fluorescent light. What are they hurrying to when it's so late that everything else is shut? A food stall for supper? The scene is familiar—two friends out for the evening—but a suggestion of danger lurks as if some act is about to be committed, or maybe just was. The men's walk is urgent; their shoulders incline forward, pushing towards the light. Nothing is in focus. The blurriness makes us anxious, even as our eye recognizes the interplay of shadow and light as beautiful. It is with this tension that we see Comel, too. She's pretty, her clothes and make-up are colorful, she's just checking the messages on her phone. But we don't know where she is, don't know what she will be doing after she finishes writing messages. We don't know if she will be safe.

■

A few weeks ago, I drove out to the Selangor coastline, to Port Klang and beyond. I wanted to see the cheap seafood joints and goat farms I remembered from my childhood, not out of any pronounced sense of nostalgia, but just to see how things had changed in the twenty-odd years since I'd last been there. There were more palm oil plantations than before, though I couldn't be sure. The people working there seemed now to be almost entirely drawn from migrant workers, and they seemed to have more tools, their uniforms indicating a greater degree of organization and industry than the casual labor of two decades ago. I didn't recognize any landmarks, and couldn't in the end find the crab shacks my parents had taken me to. They probably don't exist anymore. But these changes didn't alter the nature of the landscape—small wooden boats lay marooned on the mud flats of the rivers when the tide was out, as they did before; derelict-looking shacks full of pieces of scrap stood under the broad spread of acacia trees; coffee shops that hadn't been renovated for years continued to draw in a few customers; the small towns I drove through seemed busy and—as always—on the verge of shutdown.

I stopped for iced coffee in a place by the side of the road, a shack not unlike the one in Ian's series of photographs. On one side of it lay a tire repair shop, on the other a muddy parking lot half-filled with stacks of concrete slabs. I overheard a conversation in Cantonese—two men in their thirties talking about jobs and girls. They wanted to work in Kuala Lumpur, and then maybe Hong Kong, or China—China was where the action was these days. One of them had had a fling with a girl from Shenzhen, China, but he thought maybe she was a hooker. He was wearing a t-shirt that said "Texas Country" above a drawing of a racing car.

In my mind's eye, I always saw the Selangor coastline as somewhere fixed, unchanging, but it was never so. I had just been too young to see that the sea brought with it not just goods but people, and that made it easy for people to leave, too. In my imagination this was somewhere that would never change—the buildings would always be rundown, the towns would never acquire the gloss of Kuala Lumpur, the people would forever be dockworkers and farmers. It was unchanging in its foreignness, its difference from me. Yet in its conception and its evolution, it represents exactly the arc of Malaysian society. It tells, starkly, the tale of migration, both of arrival and departure, and of carving out a place in the world. In the flimsy roadside restaurants and old timber village houses I saw how the buildings anticipate the passing of things, but also how the temporary has a strange habit of becoming permanent.

Claire-Louise Bennett

Claire-Louise Bennett is the author of *Pond* (2015), a work difficult to define although it is most often described as a collection of twenty short stories. A series of essays, a novel, or letters could also describe the work. "*Pond* is the way it is," Claire-Louise told an interviewer for the *Paris Review*, "because of the way I am, more or less." *Pond* responds to "atmosphere much more than plot . . . and it seems it gathers much more effectively around a lone voice, just like it does around a single candle flame perhaps." The subjunctive qualifiers also dominate the style of *Fish Out of Water*—a book-length essay on Dorothea Tanning, merging her and her subject's autobiographies. This essay is an earlier version of *Fish Out of Water*, written in a sparser, critical style, and published in *Frieze* magazine. It twins Bennett and Tanning's strange nocturnal melees—a state Tanning painted onto canvas fifty years before Bennett comes to her for consolation. Both are strange essays, reading more like fiction than criticism, and reading Bennett's essay as someone who is *not* Tanning feels as if I am reading her most intimate diary. More than a conversation between writer and artist, in Tanning, Bennett recognizes a burning fire, a "striking and intimate similarity," a "kindredness," a promise "that perhaps seeing you, through the metamorphosis of your rupturing canvases and fugacious sculptures, would show me something—would in fact restore to me that essential source which had become so small and distant and faded." The rush of Bennett's long, intensely punctuated paragraphs wend and build, accumulating across pages and pages, searching for something—consolation? Redemption? Recognition?—as if, as she says, "trying to give myself the slip." In Bennett's rolling, oceanic prose, one can hear echoes of Tanning herself, as if ventriloquized. In this room in *Museo Reina Sofía*, lit by light both "dim and restful," Tanning's "languid yet attentive biomorphic forms" ask Bennett "How come you've got so hung up on what the rest of the world is doing? Why have you turned your back on what you are made of?"

How Paint and Perception Collide in the Work of Late Surrealist Dorothea Tanning

In my favorite novel by Javier Marías, an opera singer recounts a dream—a dream that is very similar to a fateful episode that occurred during his waking hours some four years previously. In order to recall what happened and the dream of what happened, the two versions must remain indistinguishable from each other and, to this end, he selects to forgo breakfast. Our entranced narrator has read somewhere that by avoiding food we can delay contact with the day and its diminishing effect on our reveries. "It is only through the second awakening, that of the stomach, that you can entirely leave behind you the darkness and the nocturnal realm,"[1] he writes. Here in Madrid, Marías's birthplace, I have, night after night, been set upon by rancorous dreams, brought on no doubt by the passionate hatred I feel almost immediately towards anything I manage to write. I wake at 6:37 am with the feeling my skin has come loose, is sliding down my stark, undulating limbs, and my hair is a nasty wig, wayward with static. The leering visitations continue needling me from head to toe, even as I lie there with cold, wide-open eyes, like an exemplary surrealist decomposition.

I will go to her today, I think, one morning, still dark, spat out again at 6:37 am. The night detests me and the day is mostly disdainful. There is nothing else for it. I will go to her just like this, haunted and scant. My etiolated mind nothing more than a rattled, thin disc, butting fruitlessly against my cranium. Remembering the tormented opera singer's considered abstinence, I too eschew my morning repast to stay close to the caliginous carousel of bone-picking phantoms. Let us all go together dammit, my gnarly shades and I, to the one place in this city where we might find some peace. I dress carefully, of course—mustn't look slipshod; she has a keen eye for fabric, for folds, after all. Well-turned-out, perhaps, but far from pulled together. Beneath that pristine white shirt and boutique animal-print skirt it is a capsizing, self-defeating body that lopes down the streets of Madrid towards Dorothea Tanning. A motley flock of sniping night revilers vexing its heels.

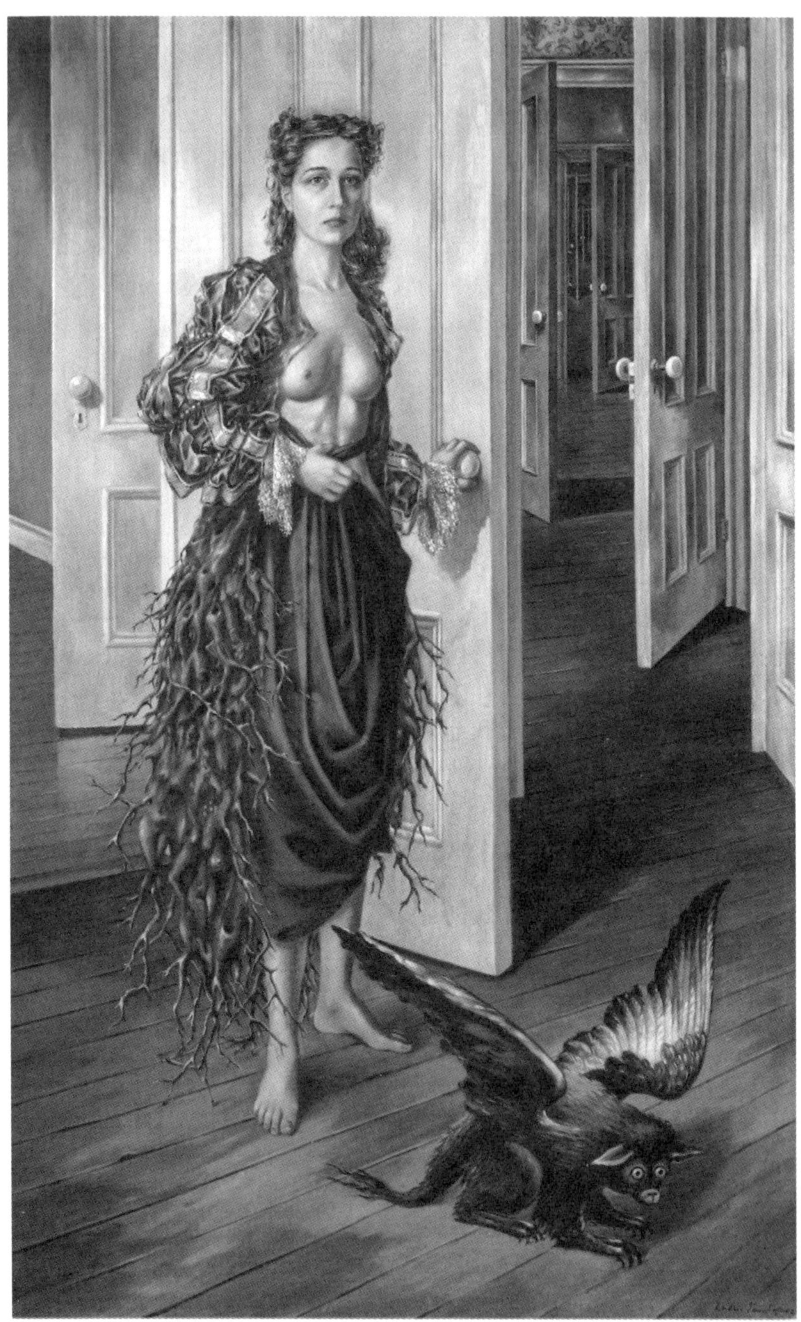

Dorothea Tanning, “Birthday,” 1942, oil on canvas, 40¼ x 25½ inches.
Courtesy of the Philadelphia Museum of Art.

And there she is, right away. The first thing in the world. And what is she wearing, exactly? The most extraordinary cloak! Its voluminous sleeves all rippling pale gold and purple silk, trimmed with intricate lace; the skirt a languorous green-gold cascade of supple seaweed bodies. Hard breasts bared, and magnificent naked feet. And her eyes! They look all the way into me and my own body unravels, threatens to spill across the floor, all green. Startled eyes dart rapidly, hither and thither, avoiding her gaze, trying to stay above water.

This arresting self-portrait, one of Tanning's first paintings, was spotted by Max Ernst in 1942. "What do you call it?" he asked. "I really haven't a title," she replied. "Then you call it *Birthday*," he said.[2] He was onto something—isn't it customary to feel a little removed from the world on one's birthday, rather than buoyant and seminal? Doesn't acknowledging we were born make us feel ephemeral, listless, arbitrary and essentially alone? Tanning stands in front of a receding avenue of open doors, fingers firm around the handle of the nearest one, looking as if she is about to push it closed, but can't quite. The image upends the seasonable platitude that there is so much still to come. Here the doors are identical and heavy-looking. Instead of hinting at infinite possibility, they emphasize the apartment's immovable emptiness. An opulent but timeworn strip of wallpaper can be glimpsed, nudging the scene into a somewhat circumscribed arena of opportunity—and bringing to mind Tanning's summation of Galesburg, Illinois, her birthplace, where "nothing happened but the wallpaper."[3] In the portrait's foreground, a winged lemur crouches at the artist's feet, a fantastical creature associated with nighttime and the spirit world. Its arched and tinted open wings extend a far more beguiling invitation. The pack of phantasms inside me lurch and ruffle excitedly—she is looking at me, and evidently the lemur has spotted them. We have found our familiars. Onwards, then.

In the next room, I discover a glass case containing a couple of letters, edged with airy, almost cartoonish, sketches, which Tanning wrote to Joseph Cornell from Arizona. Following a nasty virus that required a long period of recovery, she and Ernst moved to the desert in 1946. In her memoir, *Between Lives* (2001), Tanning refers, in characteristically protean fashion, to "the pure excitement of living in such a place of ambivalent elements." She corresponded regularly with Cornell during the three years she lived in Sedona. It's lovely to peer down at her handwriting, to decipher the faded, cobwebby script. "My dreams, my illusory impressions and my waking life are all so mixed and confusing," she writes, "that I sometimes wonder if there is any reality at all." Born amidst a storm in 1910, Tanning's psyche was perhaps destined to be perennially charged and overturned by "unknown forces." Drawn to fairy tales and gothic literature as a child, Tanning delighted in mystery and surprise. It is small wonder that the surrealist predilection for the unconscious, dreams, irrationality, chance and startling incongruities had such a galvanizing effect on her already boundless personal and artistic vision. "Here is the infinitely faceted world I must have been waiting for," was her reaction on seeing the exhibition "Fantastic Art, Dada, Surrealism" at New York's Museum of Modern Art in 1936, "but here, here in the museum, is the real explosion, rocking me over my run-over heels."

In an adjoining room, *Eine Kleine Nachtmusik* (1943) looms. This striking and disquieting work also makes use of a series of identical doors. Here they are numbered; perhaps we are in a hotel. There on the crimson landing are two little girls. One is confronting the enormous torn and avid head of a sunflower; her serpentine hair screeches upward, tiny fists are clenched. The other rests against a door jamb as if in a swoon, the bright petal swinging in her hand, a kind of keepsake. It's a peculiar canvas, somehow airless, yet arousing an unnerving impulse for violence. *Run at that flickering seedbed, little girl, run at it and pounce on it and pummel it to an oily pulp with those determined little fists*. Tanning revealed in a 1999 letter that the sunflower, a cyclopic bloom common in Galesburg, is "a symbol of all the things that youth has to face and to deal with." Inspired by the Comte de Lautréamont's *Les Chants de Maldoror* (The Songs of Maldoror, 1869) and his notion of beauty as the "chance encounter of a sewing machine and an umbrella on an operating table," the juxtaposition of deracinated and disparate symbols became a distinguishing feature of the surrealist tableau. The rich illogical dreamscapes of free association enabled Tanning to explore her treasure trove of personal icons and enduring preoccupations, thereby giving full expression to her childhood imagination and its innately eclectic catalogue of fears, fantasies and domestic psychodramas.

From an early age, Tanning felt that "an exceptional destiny"[4] awaited her, yet she was marooned in a cosseted world of pecan pies, lazy-daisy quilts, cone-shaped paper cups, fluffy afternoon dresses, Sunday cigars and too-tight satin shoes. In her essay, "Dorothea Tanning and Her Gothic Imagination" (2011), art historian Victoria Carruthers notes: "Motifs from childhood are never very far away from those early works. The iconography of the confined interior as a stage where events lead to a kind of liberation of the imagination is repeated over and over."[5] A keen eye for quotidian detail; a restless imagination and a taste for high drama; a desperate need to peel away the wallpaper and broaden her horizons; Carruthers suggests that the tensions between these potent aspects of Tanning's burgeoning inner world produced a gothic sensibility that brought the claustrophobic hub of everyday life and the outer edges of desire and dread into terrifying and exuberant proximity. Shortly before her death, talking to Carruthers about her penchant for gothic fantasy, Tanning said: "It allowed the possibility of creating a new reality, one not dependent on bourgeois values but a way of showing what was actually happening under the tedium of daily life."

Contemplating the gothic dimension in Tanning's work, its particular mode of disrupting the boundary between reality and fantasy, provides some insight into what drew her towards surrealism. It might also help us appreciate why she began to rub up against the paradoxical limits of its variegated techniques. Reflecting on this seismic stylistic shift, Tanning writes: "I began to chafe just a little at the reliance on precisely painted elements of the natural world in order to present an incongruity ... everything was *collage*."[6] While the surrealist meetings continued in Paris in the 1950s, where she and Ernst were living at the time, Tanning's impatience was simmering: "Gradually, in looking at how many ways paint can flow onto canvas, I began to long for letting it have more freedom."[7] Something more vital was pushing at the surface: "Around 1955, my canvases literally splintered."[8] Loosened from the pristine motifs of surrealism, no longer bound to figurative precision, Tanning used paint to convey the flux of immediate experience. At this crucial point, Carruthers argues, "Tanning disbands her desire to portray the gothic as if she were illustrating a gothic tale, in favour of evoking the gothic sensibility of fracture and fragmentation through abstraction."

The results are beyond sensuous—paint and perception collide, these canvases are not secretive, hypnagogic depictions of the past, they are dynamic and embodied expressions of the present. *Melées nocturnes* (Nocturnal Melees, 1958) is a glinting cavern of subterranean seeresses. It emanates a sanguine tenderness that is both visceral and cabbalistic. Confronting it, something slack and gaping below my last rib on the left side exalts. The eyes in my head, it seems, are hardly doing any of the seeing here. I turn again, and there is *Même les jeunes filles* (Even the Young Girls, 1966). My eyes struggle to bring into focus this tumult of ecstatic entities, yet some other part of me is already communing with them. They are all over each other; I am giddy and transfixed. The canvases thrum with an Artaudian liveness. "I wanted to lead the eye into spaces that hid, revealed, transformed all at once and where there would be some never-before-seen image, as if it had appeared with no help from me."[9] These are not so much paintings as organisms, with an intelligence of their own. When you look at one, it's as if your glance has caught it in the middle of a calm yet seminal activity. "You coax the picture out of its cage," wrote Tanning, "along with personae, essences, its fatidic suggestion, its insolence. Friend or enemy?"[10]

In a letter to Cornell in 1948, Tanning wrote that she believed there is only poetry and revulsion. What she'd like to do, she revealed, is "let the poetry in and keep the revulsion out." She tells Cornell that he manages to do that in his work, and she wonders how. "I wish I were not so aware of what the rest of the world is doing," she confesses. "Maybe that is your secret, maybe that is what you keep out." What becomes clear as I move through this body of work that spans more than 70 years is that, although Tanning was very much engaged with the world and its people, her creative practice was directed by her own concerns, obsessions, instincts and pleasures. "It was, after all, your hand, your will, your turmoil that has produced it all, this brand-new event in a very old world."[11] I come to stand in a room of soft sculptures. The light is dim and restful in here, the languid yet attentive biomorphic forms gently picked out by diffuse spotlights. I've looked at each shape in turn and now I just want to be in their company, in their world, and experience their strange consoling presence. I hear them murmur: "How come you've got so hung up on what the rest of the world is doing? Why have you turned your back on what you are made of?" Because I've been shaken down and emptied out by the nagging feeling that I ought to come up with something entirely different from what I've written before. The nauseating wrong-headedness of this notion has made itself apparent as I've crept and spun through this psychical hall of mirrors, which has shown me that creative energy is a naturally evolving force, giving rise, always, to "another of the thousand ways of saying the same thing."[12] Scornful and despairing of my treasure trove, I've been keeping a firm lid on it—is it any wonder then that the essences within have turned on me, and wreak havoc in the dark hours? Friend or enemy? Shade, or vital spark? This morning, I have nourished my spurned fundamentals. They fold into me, sated and aligned. Now it is time for me to eat, to awaken the stomach; it is time to face the day.

Notes

1. Javier Marías, *The Man of Feeling*, trans. Margaret Jull Costa (New York: Vintage Books, 2003), 32.
2. Dorothea Tanning, *Birthday* (Santa Monica: The Lapis Press, 1986), 14.
3. Dorothea Tanning, *10 Recent Paintings and a Biography* (New York: Gimpel-Weitzenhoffer Gallery, 1979), 2. Exhibition catalog.
4. Tanning, *10 Recent Paintings*, 5.
5. Victoria Carruthers, "Dorothea Tanning and Her Gothic Imagination," *Journal of Surrealism and the Americas* 5, no.1 (2011): 144–45.
6. Dorothea Tanning, *Between Lives: An Artist and Her World* (Evanston: Northwestern University Press, 2001), 213.
7. Tanning, *Between Lives*, 213.
8. Tanning, 178.
9. Tanning, 214.
10. Tanning, 325.
11. Tanning, 326.
12. Tanning, 178.

Teju Cole

Teju Cole is a novelist, essayist, critic, and photographer. His four major publications—his debut novel, *Open City* (2011); his novella-cum-travelogue, *Every Day Is for the Thief* (2014); *Known and Strange Things* (2016), an expansive body of critical essays covering political, literary, and aesthetic subjects; and the published companion to his major 2016 photographic exhibition, *Blind Spot* (first published in Italian as *Punto d'Ombra*, then in English in 2017)—have been described by the author himself as "a quartet of books about the limits of vision." But as a trained art historian and celebrated photographer, Cole is as prominent in the world of visual art as he is in the world of letters. From 2015 until 2019, he wrote a monthly column "On Photography" for the *New York Times Magazine*. "There's Less to Portraits Than Meets the Eye, and More" is a piece from this time. His artistic practice thrives in the intervallic territory between the literary and visual arts: a writer and photographer, he has recently taken on the roles of performance artist, Instagram innovator, and Spotify virtuoso, documenting aural moodscapes in playlists such as "A History of Jetlag" and "27 Roads," inspired by Robert Adams's photographic ode to the road. In an interview with Patrick Marschke, Cole argued that such collaborative performances "respond . . . to something other than the needs of the exigencies of the marketplace"—a space of artistic innovation and improvisation where "some other thing can happen." When looking at a photograph by American photographer Dawoud Bey in "There's Less to Portraits Than Meets the Eye, and More," Cole's slow and considered observational style produces prose like the incoming tide. Considering the photograph "Young Man at a Tent Revival, Brooklyn, NY, 1989," he notes the pull of physiognomy: "I want to fall back on old ways and say that the gentle arch of the boy's left eyebrow seems to mark him as an ironic sort, or that the symmetry of his features make him both trusting and trustworthy. But really, that would be projecting." What can we tell from a face? Deeply invested in an ethics of care, the portrait is an exemplar of this: it "is an open door. It can remind us of our ethical duty to the other."

There's Less to Portraits Than Meets the Eye, and More

Portraiture existed long before photography was invented. And for more than a dozen years after photography's invention, it was practically impossible to make a photographic portrait: the required exposure times were too long. But the two eventually came together, and now their pairing seems so natural that it's as though photography was invented for making portraits.

One of the first photographic portraits, if not the first, was a self-portrait daguerreotype made by a 30-year-old amateur chemist from Philadelphia named Robert Cornelius. Cornelius held his pose for several minutes in the bright October sun in 1839. His dark coat has a high collar, and his hair is tousled. The catalog text at the Library of Congress adds that he is "peering uncertainly into the camera." But is that true? How would we verify it?

We tend to interpret portraits as though we were reading something inherent in the person portrayed. We talk about strength and uncertainty; we praise people for their strong jaws and pity them their weak chins. High foreheads are deemed intelligent. We easily link the people's facial features to the content of their character. This is odd. After all, we no longer believe you can determine someone's personality by measuring their skull with a pair of calipers. Phrenology has rightly been consigned to the dustbin of history. But physiognomy, the idea that faces carry meanings, still haunts the interpretation of portraiture.

The reason for the temptation is obvious: faces are malleable. A smile is intentional and might indeed indicate happiness, just as a furrowed brow might be proof of a melancholic temperament. But we also know that emotion is fleeting and can be faked. We thus shouldn't really trust whatever it is a photographic portrait seems to be telling us.

This is not to deny any of the wonder or gratitude you feel before a superb portrait. Sometimes this response is amplified when it's a portrait of someone not famous, a face that isn't burdened with predetermined knowledge. I'm looking at one such image in Dawoud Bey's magnificent career retrospective, *Seeing Deeply* (2018). In the book, this black-and-white photograph is given a full page. The format invites contemplation, and this should be mentioned because what we see in a photograph is connected to its material circumstances: an exhibition print of the same image would give one impression, a magazine reproduction would be another, a digital file meant to be seen on a computer or hand-held device is something else again. The warm tone and low gloss of this photograph in this book are calming. A boy stands alone before a tent and some chairs. We don't know who he is, and the caption doesn't help much: "Young Man at a Tent Revival, Brooklyn, NY, 1989." The surprising detail there is the date, as this picture looks as if it could have been taken at any point in the past century. It is strangely timeless, with his attire somewhere between formal and casual, the slim dark tie and serious black pants contrasting with the baggy pale-colored plaid shirt.

I want to fall back on old ways and say that the gentle arch of the boy's left eyebrow seems to mark him as an ironic sort, or that the symmetry of his features make him both trusting and trustworthy. But really, that would be projecting. What we can really say is that there's something poignant about the way the skinny tie is tucked into the skinny belt and the way the numerous verticals in the picture—the tent poles, the ropes of its rigging, the legs of the chairs in the background, the tie, the lines of the shirt and finally the boy himself—all seem to be tilting just off true.

The picture wavers in tremulous equilibrium. Even the boy's head is cocked to the side. Quizzically? Or is he simply at his ease? I don't know. But the cumulative effect is endearing. There's a boy, and his appearance is dense with a life that we can only guess at. There's faith in it (it's a revival, after all); there's probably hope, too. But what we can be surer of is that there's love: the love with which Dawoud Bey has seen the elements of the moment and captured them for posterity, and the love with which, almost three decades later, I am looking at this portrait in a book.

■

The rise of portrait photography made immortality of a new kind available to ordinary people. Picture-making establishments in New York, Boston and San Francisco displayed countless photographs of seamstresses, servants, soldiers, laborers, lawyers and even the recently dead. A wide swath of society owned treasured likenesses of themselves that they displayed at home, kept in specially made cases, sent to their lovers or bequeathed to their descendants. And that abundance has become, in our time, positively torrential. There must be very few people on Earth who have not been photographed.

But something truly strange has also happened: automation is playing an outsize role in the creation and dissemination of photographic portraits. Machines are making images of people for other machines to see and analyze. We are photographed when we cross international borders. Cameras in public places scan and collect the faces of passers-by. We rouse our mobile phones with our faces. Even the cameras on our computers cannot be trusted not to spy on us. Our faces are spirited away in the name of societal stability, crime prevention, corporate profit or national security.

Surveillance is nothing new, but with storage getting cheaper and analytical tools more ferocious, a dystopian future is closer than it has ever been. In many parts of China, ubiquitous facial data collection is already an everyday reality. Facial-recognition technology is giving the government there powerful tools to control and discipline its populace. Unsurprisingly, religious minorities and political activists, in addition to petty offenders and hardened criminals, are already bearing the brunt of these initiatives. To be ethnically Uighur in China today, for example, is to be under tremendous restriction. Other governments will follow, and arguments about the right to privacy or freedom will lag behind.

Machines take advantage of the particularity of each person's appearance to flatten out our collective individuality. A machine sees without sympathy. And yet our individual particularities might themselves serve as a comfort in this machine-driven age. The shape of my lips, the shine on my nose, the corners of my eyes, the breadth of my forehead: the same features that allow machines to track me are also dear to the people who love me (not because those features are objectively special but because they are mine). And those features also say something to people who don't know me: that I am not disembodied, that I am not abstraction. Physiognomy is of limited use: I am not my face. But a set of features retains affect, as in a cistern, and from this something more subtle can be retrieved.

A photographic portrait records a human encounter. The photographer's intent and the sitter's agreement, and vice versa, are made visible. The portrait also contains the tacit hope that a third party, the viewer, will be able to register the traces of that previous encounter. Better if it's printed out and held in the hand, vibrant to the touch. This was the experience of those who bought the small, inexpensive cardboard-mounted photographs known as *cartes de visite* in the 19th century.

Perhaps the most famous usage of the American *carte de visite* was by Sojourner Truth, in the 1860s. Truth escaped from slavery in Ulster County, New York, in 1826 and became a noted abolitionist activist. She was a gifted orator who, as one contemporary noted, "poured forth a torrent of natural eloquence which swept everything before it." Illiteracy did not prevent her from producing (with the help of intermediaries) a large number of letters, speeches, petitions and autobiographical texts. And, particularly during the years of the Civil War, she also sat for numerous photographers, leaving behind at least 28 different photographs. Most of these were printed as *cartes de visite* and sold to support her abolitionist work.

One of the senses of "shadow" at that time was "photograph," and from 1864 onward, Truth's *cartes de visite* included a caption text and her name: "I Sell the Shadow to Support the Substance. Sojourner Truth." She was not the photographer of these images, but so insistent was her control over how she was seen that these are practically self-portraits.

Like Frederick Douglass (with whom she had a mutual antipathy), Truth knew how powerful a photographic presence could be in the struggle to make white Americans see Black American humanity. Her photograph was not herself—it was a shadow, and as an ex-slave that distinction must have been one she sensed especially keenly—but she knew it did convey some indelible news of her reality. The photos show a tall and somewhat gaunt woman in her 60s, in modest dress and with a white shawl and cap, sometimes sitting, sometimes standing. Her skin is dark and smooth, and her expression might be read either as serious or neutral. Though she tends to look directly at the camera, her eyes are usually obscured behind glasses. Truth's photographs did not have the cosmopolitan and occasionally conceited air that Douglass's did but, like his, they reminded others that

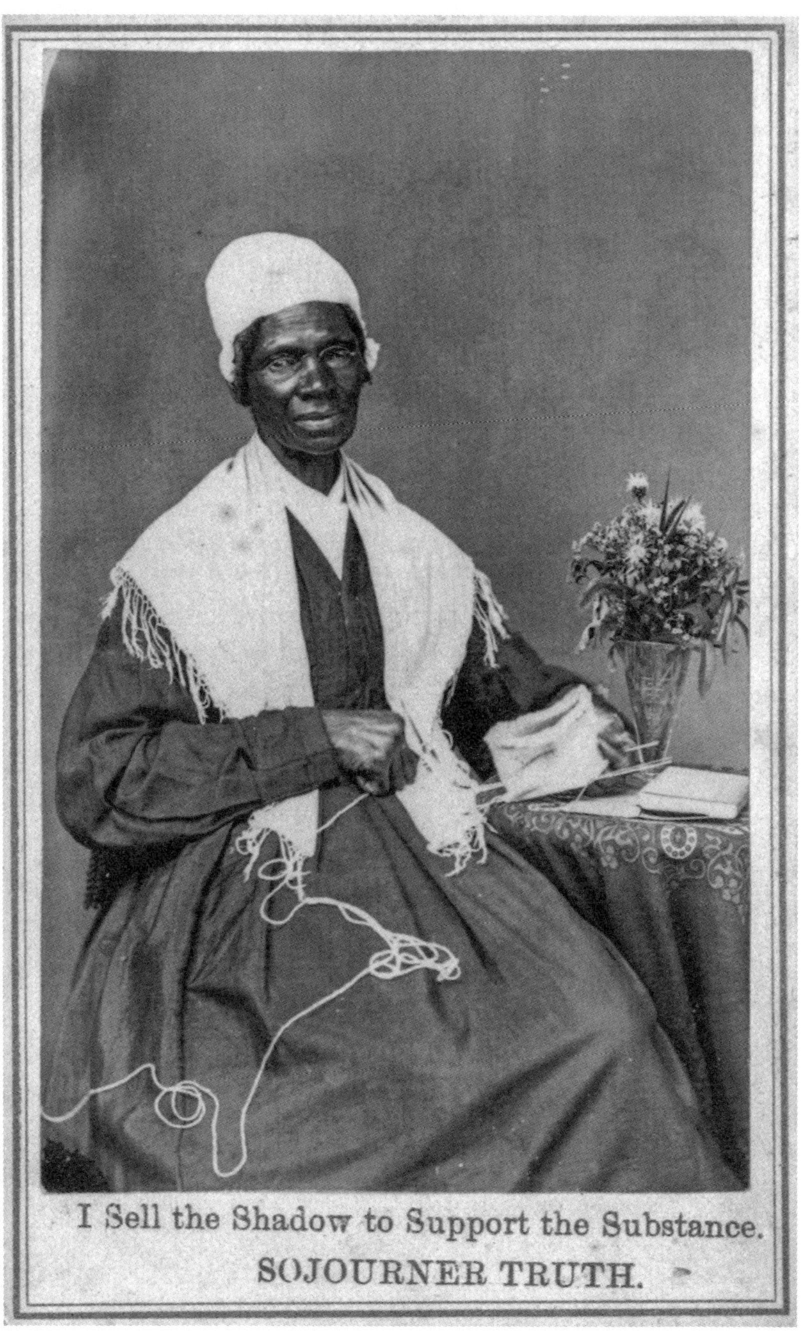

Carte de visite of Sojourner Truth, around 1864.
Courtesy of the American Antiquarian Society.

she did have a real self and that her dignity was not negotiable, and this reminder was a challenge to the conscience of all who saw, held or bought the "shadow."

A portrait is an open door. It can remind us of our ethical duty to the other. "The face speaks to me, and thereby invites me to a relation," as the philosopher Emmanuel Lévinas puts it. Unlike machines, we see with sympathy. (This is why a mere portrait of a despot can be dangerously effective propaganda. The portrait humanizes the person depicted in ways we can't quite control. Inhuman behavior is rarely apparent on a human face.) A photograph by Berenice Abbott, Seydou Keïta, Gordon Parks, Dawoud Bey or any of the greats in the history of photography, a portrait of Sojourner Truth, Frederick Douglass or an unnamed boy standing in front of a tent in Brooklyn presents us with the face of the other and restores us to ourselves. Some magic happens there, a magic as old and reliable as the portraits painted on the Fayyum funerary boards 2,000 years ago. Not all portraits are created equal: to be great, they must contain presence, tension, a finely balanced amalgam of feeling and craft. "This is human," is the final meaning of a great portrait, "and I am human, and this is worth defending."

Geoff Dyer

Geoff Dyer is a prolific cultural critic whose nineteen books regularly flout or vex generic constraints. Emblematic is 1991's *But Beautiful,* a series of literary vignettes about jazz musicians inspired by photographs, grounded in biography, but unashamedly fictionalizing his subjects' lives—a format that he continued to develop in *The Ongoing Moment* (2005), an alternative photographic history in which Dyer stages imagined conversations between some of the form's greatest artists. Reflecting on the writing of *But Beautiful,* Dyer notes that when he began, he "was unsure of the form it should take. This was a great advantage since it meant I had to improvise and so, from the start, the writing was animated by the defining characteristic of its subject." Before long, he found he "had moved away from anything like conventional criticism," and describes his writing as "as much *imaginative criticism* as fiction." Dyer's serious critical work on photography is counterbalanced by peaks of delightful surprise: "now we shall see!"; "a documentary record of documents!" We see this most in his analysis of Dayanita Singh's work of photographic fiction *Dream Villa,* where he works against the grain of critical practice, arguing "the way to understand this picture is by reversing into it, as it were, by the *opposite* of storytelling." There isn't "a mystery that will be revealed if we scrutinize the picture closely enough." Instead, "what we see here is a demonstration of photography's ability to depict a state of negative capability."

Now We Can See

Arriving at Indira Gandhi International Airport in 2006, I was confronted by an unusually impressive advertisement. It featured a big and grainy black-and-white photograph of the tabla player Zakir Hussain and his dad Ustad Alla Rakha in concert, some time in the mid-1980s, I guessed. Zakir's dad is reaching over and patting his son's head, ruffling his hair as if to congratulate the puppy on having barked with such enthusiastic promise. But, with this loving gesture, the preeminent tabla player of one generation—in the famous concert for Bangladesh it's the grinning Alla Rakha we see accompanying Ravi Shankar on sitar and Ali Akbar Khan on sarod—is also passing on the musical baton to the man Bill Laswell will later describe as "the greatest rhythm player that this planet has ever produced."[1] Quite a claim!

The picture turned out to be by Dayanita Singh, who, in one of the little home-made-looking photographic journals from the box set *Sent a Letter* (Steidl, 2008), has constructed a tribute to her mum: a passing back of something that was never quite a baton. The other six books in the set take their names from places in India—"Calcutta," "Bombay" and so on—whereas this one, with its slightly darker cover, is named after Dayanita's mother, Nony Singh. It's made up of either pictures Nony took or of ones she—Nony—found in her husband's cupboard. There are quite a few pictures of a little girl with a determined little pout or frowning smile who is clearly Dayanita.

Is that smile-pout a precocious sign of ambition? When the 18-year-old Dayanita first went to photograph Hussain at a concert the organizers tried to prevent her and she tripped over. Embarrassed but undeterred she called out, "Mr. Hussain, I am a young student today, but someday I will be an important photographer, and then we will see."[2] Mr. Hussain liked this spirited response and allowed the student to travel with him and his fellow musicians, to document his life on the road and at home. The picture at Delhi airport was from *Zakir Hussain* (Himalayan Books, 1986), the book that resulted from this—Dayanita's first.

Now that her injured boast has been made good, another kind of continuity can be seen. It too can be illustrated musically. Many of the greatest living female singers of the Karnatic and Hindustani classical traditions are in their sixties or seventies. As they take slowly to the stage they look magisterial, imposing, grand—conscious of the immensity of their reputations. It can take them a while to get seated, cross-legged, but when these ladies start to sing the years fall away to reveal a lovely girlishness. A part of time has been stopped. Their voices are light-footed and graceful as the *gopis* spied upon by Krishna—but with the knowledge, wisdom and, often, sadness of age. Now look again at that set of diaries, *Sent a Letter*: in its high-art-home-spun way, it's not unlike the kind of thing you might have tried to make as a kid in art classes—and it's as far removed from a super-sized Andreas Gursky or Thomas Struth as one could get. *Go Away Closer* (Steidl, 2007) looks like a school exercise book. The book of *Dream Villa* photographs (Steidl, 2010)—many of them printed quite large in exhibitions—seems intended to pass itself off as a pocket diary. This last, in my view, is a perverse decision and major aesthetic mistake—what is the gain in having the double-page, full-bleed spreads dominated by the gutter?—but the general point stands: playfulness, pleasure in the possibilities of the modest and the miniature, are not at odds with seriousness; they are part of what enabled Dayanita to become "an important photographer."

While it was perfectly natural for Zakir to become a tabla player—as Martin Amis says somewhere, there's nothing more normal than what your dad does—there were numerous obstacles to be overcome if the young student was to turn her mum's hobby into a vocation and profession. These were obstacles born of expectation: what was expected of young women in India and what was expected from Indian photographers and photographs of India generally. With Dayanita's work there is a subtle but clear break from the teeming streets of Raghu Rai and the crowd of colors associated with Raghubir Singh, in favor of a photography that is quiet, intimate, private, withdrawn: an art, increasingly, of absence.

In one of the pictures by her mum, the baby Dayanita is barely visible; in a couple of others she is entirely overlooked in favor of a hotel room. The grown-up daughter has followed suit; her pictures are full of empty rooms, empty beds and what Billy Collins calls "the chairs that no one sits in": "where no one/is resting a glass or placing a book facedown."[3] The poet is here thinking of permanently empty—rather than briefly vacated—chairs, but in photography, of course, even the momentary becomes permanent. And in photographic terms, these empty chairs have always been with us. Or at least, as John Szarkowski, former Director of Photography at MoMA argues, they did not mean "the same thing before photography as they mean to us now."[4]

About half of the pictures in *Privacy* (Steidl, 2004) are portraits of people in their opulent homes—spacious rooms crowded with wealth and flesh. The effect of these is to make the other half, the empty interiors, seem … even emptier! And then there are the museum rooms of Anand Bhavan (now Swaraj Bhavan), the former Nehru family residence in Allahbad, where we get a redoubled, much-multiplied emptiness: unworn clothes hanging on the unopened doors of empty rooms. The glaring absence in these pictures, these rooms, is of the present (as symbolized by the stilled ceiling fan). This is what time looks like after history has moved on and left it for dead.

Referring to his own photographs of empty interiors, Walker Evans once said, "I do like to suggest people sometimes by their absence. I like to make you feel that an interior is *almost* inhabited by somebody."[5] The dominant suggestion in Dayanita's rooms is not so much of the absence of people so much as the *lack* of their absence: the idea of people, I mean, doesn't rush in to fill the vacancy. The wide-awake day bed, the armchair never passing up a chance to take the weight off its feet, the books wanting nothing more than to curl up with a good book—all are perfectly content with the prospect of an evening on their own, undisturbed by human intrusion.

What Dayanita shares with Evans is the ability to suggest another, rarer, absence: that of the photographer. Making it seem that the room itself had done the photographing was Evans's paradoxical and signature gift: the air of anonymity—"the non-appearance of the author," as he put it—that enables us to identify an Evans *as* an Evans.[6] In this he both expressed an ideal—of the photographer disappearing into his photographs—and harked back to the dawn of the medium, to William Henry Fox Talbot's claim about an image made in 1836: "this building I believe to be the first that was ever yet known *to have drawn its own picture*."[7]

The silent atmosphere of places surveying themselves pervades Dayanita's rooms, corridors and halls. It's at its most extreme in a picture of (so extreme it seems more appropriate to write "picture *by*") the library in Anand Bhavan (*Visitors at Anand Bhavan, Allahbad*, 2000). There *are* people in this photograph—visitors peering in through the glass that preserves and isolates the room—but the sense of latent sentience is so strong that a kind of role reversal occurs: as if the room itself is regarding a vitrine displaying these time-frozen specimens of life-sized humanity.

Elsewhere this sense is enhanced and signaled by the way that the rooms often contain other photographs, either actual ones—hanging on walls, propped on shelves—or, less tangibly, in the form of reflections: in shining floors and polished furnishings, in windows and mirrors. (It's often impossible, in photographs, to tell the difference between a mirror and a photo. In a photo, in fact, a mirror is automatically transformed *into* a photo. A photo, let's say, is a mirror with the time taken out of it.) The effect of these layers of self-seeing—inanimate, passive and abiding—is a cumulative laying bare of essence: the stillness of still photography. That's one way of seeing and putting it. Another, by a visitor to the 2007 exhibition of the *Go Away Closer* photographs, at the Kriti Gallery in Varanasi, was to copy into the visitors' book some lines in Urdu from a *ghazal* by Faiz Ahmad Faiz called "Hum Dekhenge" ("We Will See"):

All that will remain is Allah's Name,
He who is absent but present too,
We who is the seer as well as the seen.

Light stares whitely through the windows. These windows reflect on the interiors—as we have seen—and provide visual access to the world outside. What happens when we gaze through them? What do we see?

To answer this we first have to re-familiarize ourselves with the terrain—get an overview of how the documentary impulse in early series such as *I Am As I Am* (started in 1999) and *Myself Mona Ahmed* (1989–2001) gradually softens to something less anchored directly in place and time. Bear in mind, also, that the divisions between Dayanita's projects and books have never been absolute. A picture from *Go Away Closer* also appears in *Sent a Letter* and again in *Privacy*, and so on. The piles and shelves of documents in the recent *File Room* (Steidl, 2013) are prefigures by the libraries and piled-up books and lockers of *Privacy*. Effectively, then, the pictures are all the time overlooking each other, glancing over each other's shoulders. You can, in other words, glance out of the window of a tower in Devi Garh and gaze down at Padmanabhapuram. Until recently, you could be fairly certain that the place you looked out from—and at—was somewhere in India, but that's no longer the case. Come to think of it, a place might not even be a place—just a wall that's nowhere in particular with the image of a photographer drawn on it.

You can tell by the face of the woman in this mural—the photographic equivalent, surely, of Dayanita's tag—that this revealed and self-observing world is constantly surprising itself. Dayanita's world seems to advance by a series of rhythmic astonishments—"Ooh, I wasn't expecting that!"—so calmly accepted that they appear almost to have been intended.

This is most noticeable in Dayanita's shift to color. Color photography famously got going in the West in the 1970s—"the early Christian era of color photography," as Joel Sternfeld fondly terms it.[8] For his part, Raghubir Singh wrote that if photography had been invented in India there would have been no need for all the theoretical handwringing and claims of heresy.[9] Dayanita, on the other hand, dutifully worked through black-and-white—from documentary and reportage to the more elliptical style of *Go Away Closer*—before lurching accidentally into color. *Blue Book* (Steidl, 2009) was the result of running out of black-and-white film on a shoot. No problem, she thought, just turn it into black-and-white later. Except this was daylight film (color-adjusted to the intensity or "color temperature" of daylight), it was after sunset, and so the contacts came out blue. This blue period was short-lived—of stark, if limited, aesthetic usefulness—but the miscalibrated rainbow beckoned, and soon she was in the midst of exactly the kind of "spontaneous color experience" proclaimed by László Moholy-Nagy.[10] Having tumbled into color as people stumble into darkness—now we shall see!—she glided into the gorgeous nocturnes of *Dream Villa*.

This move was both unexpected and unsurprising in equal measure. The very last words quoted by the tabla genius in *Zakir Hussain* look ahead to the color-trance of Dayanita's tropical oneiric: "Maybe

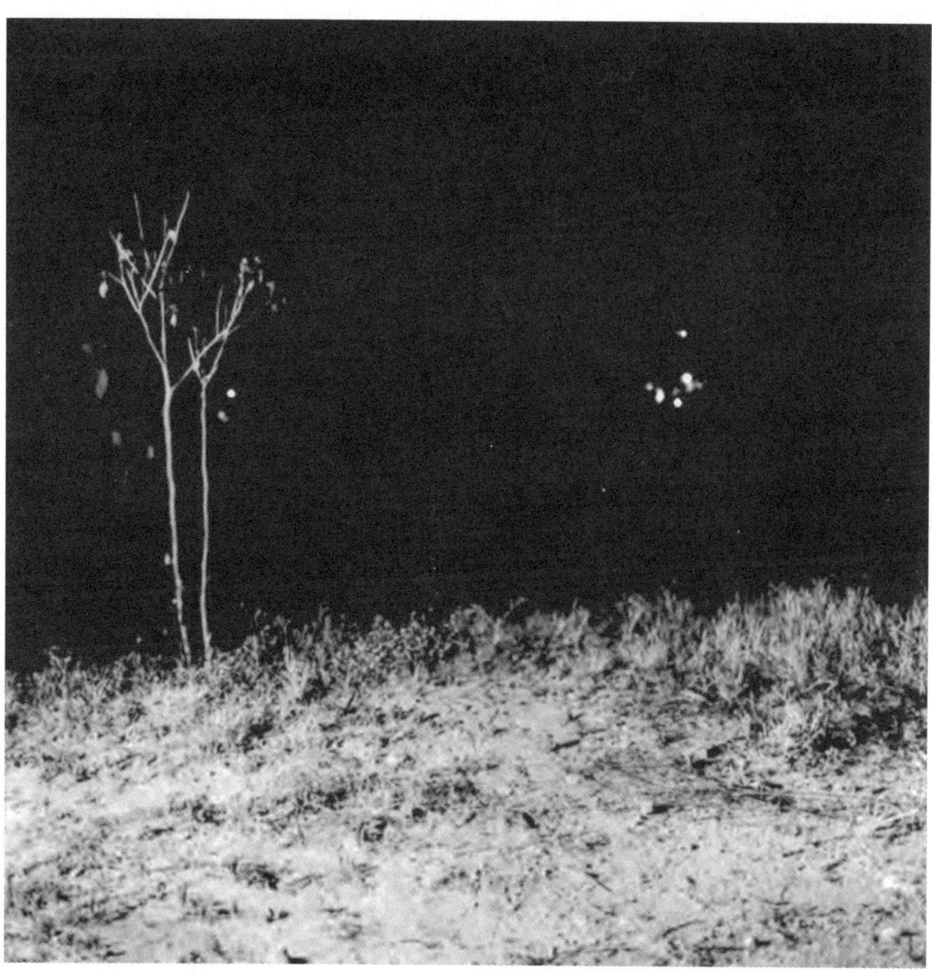

Dayanita Singh, "Red Tree (Dream Villa 44)," 2006.

it's a dream world, maybe it's make believe, but it's beautiful."[11] Either way, as Gillian Welch puts it, "she showed me colors I'd never seen."

So what makes a "Dream Villa"? How does Dayanita know she's found one? The answer, surely, is that she doesn't, or, more accurately, that the question is the answer. The *Dream Villa* pictures are all uncaptioned because the places in them don't exist. Yes, they're out there in the world somewhere and she photographs them in that interrogative way of photographers, but it's only later, when they've stopped being places and become photographs, that it's possible to see if what was once reality—or a piece of real estate, at any rate—has acquired the ideal and elusive aura of the dream image.

The image that illustrates this most vividly is of a thin tree—more twig than tree—bathed in deep red light. Michael Ackerman's first book of photographs, *End Time City* (Scalo, 1999) was obviously about an actual place: Varanasi. But in his next book, *Fiction* (Delpire, 2001), Ackerman decided he "no longer wanted to see any information in [his] pictures."[12] That's what we have here: a picture in which there is almost no information—just night, red light and trees. No before and no after, and therefore no narrative: the opposite, in a way, of an Edward Hopper painting. Wim Wenders said that Hopper always prompts us to construct little stories or movies—before-and-after scenarios: "A car will drive up to a filling station, and the driver will have a bullet in his belly."[13] It's not just that the *Dream Villa* pictures do not provoke a response of this kind; they make it seem entirely inappropriate. The red is presumably from a car's tail- or break-lights, so a car has pulled up, but that's the full extent of the story. It does not make us curious about what the car is doing there, though it does suggest that the way to understand this picture is by reversing into it, as it were, by the *opposite* of story-telling—that our curiosity will not be satisfied in narrative terms. There's not even the potential mystery of the crime that may or may not be illusory in Michelangelo Antonioni's 1966 film *Blow-Up* (although the red glow of the ground is reminiscent of the safety light in David Hemmings' darkroom), a mystery that will be revealed if we scrutinize the picture closely enough. If there is intrigue here it is in the incidental cluster of lights in the distance and over to the right: what's going on over there? There is mystery in the foreground—there is nothing *but* mystery—but not the kind that seeks an answer beyond itself. This is mysteriousness not as a goad to solving and thereby bringing the mystery to an end, but mystery as a condition in which to reside (another reason for the lack of narrative, for the lack of desire to *move on*). So it's not just stylistic clumsiness on my part that has led to this infestation of "nots"; what we see here is a demonstration of photography's ability to depict a state of negative capability.

You look at this picture without any irritable straining after truth, content in the permanence of the fleeting mystery depicted. And, when you do this, you realize that there *is* something there, in the middle of the picture. The ghost of a figure of some kind? Another tree? A mini-tornado touching harmlessly down? Just a trace of something, no more substantial than a smudge of smoke—so, perhaps that mention of the darkroom in *Blow-Up* was not as parenthetical as it seemed. What we share here is the essential mystery—in danger of post-digital extinction—and excitement, of the photographer watching an image emerge in the red glow of the darkroom. A different kind of negative capability: one that might even be a synonym for photography itself.

The colorful dissolution of the external in the *Dream Villa* series was followed by what cries out to be described as Dayanita's most "substantial" body of black-and-white work, *File Room*—a documentary record of documents! There's no room for emptiness here: sacks, cupboards, archives and cabinets are crammed full of books, papers and folders that have the weight and permanence of geological strata—minus, it goes without saying, the weight and permanence. That was an illusion—they're just pictures, after all—but how easily matters of fact become the stuff of fiction! So maybe it's not too deluded to think that if you pulled open enough drawers in one of the rooms you would find, neatly preserved and archived in some Borgesian way, *Go Away Closer, House of Love* and all the earlier books, along with the prints and contact sheets. Certainly, it seems safe to say that this, for the moment, is where Dayanita has ended up.

It's good to have things stored, stacked and available like this, to be able to go over to the shelves—organized and arranged according to some principle that only the custodian or owner understands—and pore over the relevant volumes. And then to return them, along with another more recent amendment and addition: this one.

Notes

1. Quoted by Peter Lavezzoli in *The Dawn of Indian Music in the West* (New York: Continuum, 2006), 350.
2. Dayanita Singh, *Privacy* (Göttingen: Steidl, 2004), no pagination.
3. Billy Collins, *Aimless Love: New and Selected Poems* (New York: Random House, 2013), 149.
4. John Szarkowski, *Atget* (New York: Museum of Modern Art [MoMA], 2000), 176.
5. Quoted by Belinda Rathbone in *Walker Evans: A Biography* (London: Thames & Hudson, 1995), 252.

6. Jerry L. Thompson, *Walker Evans at Work* (London: Thames & Hudson, 1984), 70.
7. William Henry Fox Talbot, "Some Account of the Art of Photogenic Drawing" (1839) in *Photography in Print*, ed. Vicki Goldberg (Albuquerque: University of New Mexico Press, 1981), 46.
8. Quoted in *Sunday Telegraph Magazine*, March 28, 2004, 29.
9. Raghubir Singh, *River of Colour: The India of Raghubir Singh* (London: Phaidon, 1998), 8.
10. László Maholy-Nagy, "Pigment to Light" (1936) in Goldberg, *Photography in Print*, 342.
11. Quoted by Dayanita Singh in *Zakir Hussain* (New Delhi: Himalayan Books, 1986), 75.
12. Michael Ackerman, *Fiction* (Paris: Delpire, 2001), no pagination.
13. Wim Wenders, *The Art of Seeing: Essays and Conversations* (London: Faber and Faber, 1996), 137.

Sheila Heti

Sheila Heti is a Canadian novelist. Already the author of *The Middle Stories* (2001) and *Ticknor* (2005), it was Heti's 2010 novel *How Should a Person Be?* that catapulted her into the critical eye, particularly on the book's revised release in the US in 2012. In this second version, Heti subtitled the work *A Novel from Life*, and has spoken at length in interviews about her disillusionment with fiction, her increased reliance on recordings of real conversations to construct her books, and the desire to create "beautiful" paintings. Heti's eclectic essays have found both mainstream and hipster forums, including the *London Review of Books*, *n+1*, the *New York Times*, *McSweeney's*, *Brooklyn Rail*, and the *Believer*. With the founding editor of the *Believer*, Heidi Julavits, and Leanne Shapton, Heti edited a collection of essays, *Women in Clothes* (2014). An attention to shopping and female identity occupies Heti in this essay, too, on the video artist Sara Cwynar. Sightly off-piste, Heti admits: "Only because in some circles I have already proven myself to be enough of an intellectual to talk publicly about art, while I have still not yet proven to *anyone* that I am the sort of woman who knows how to furnish her house with the right sort of candles." Identifying shopping as the site of difference between the artist's and the non-artist's vision, Heti also draws a distinction between the artist and the writer: "Shopping is a form of creativity. When I am writing well, I feel no need for shopping. The times in my life I have shopped a lot, it is because I have not been writing. Shopping is selecting. Writing is selecting. Shopping is choosing the best thing. Writing is choosing the best thing (the best thing to write about, and the best way of writing it)."

Should Artists Shop or Stop Shopping?

While doing research for this piece on the artist Sara Cwynar, I came across an interview which showed photographs of her studio. One of the photographs featured drippings from candles—she was melting candles, and layering the drips, and the drips would eventually be moved and put on a canvas. In a text accompanying the photograph, the journalist noted that Cwynar "tends to buy her source material from dollar stores, drug stores, eBay, and, recently, candlestock.com, a candle company based in Woodstock, New York." There was a link to candlestock.com embedded in that sentence, so I clicked on it. Then I spent ten to twenty minutes looking around candlestock.com hoping to find something to buy.

Whatever candle would end up in my house would be a symbol for me of being somehow more special and better than other people who bought their candles from Bed, Bath and Beyond, or Amazon, or Ikea, or any other place, for I had sourced my candle from an artist who used candles in her art, so clearly knew the best candle source. As I was looking at candlestock.com, it occurred to me that I didn't know which candles she bought, so she might end up with a more authentic candle than I would, while I would end up with the sort of candle of a person who was rather mediocre in her tastes, reaching for the symbol of a candle that would secretly telegraph only to *me* that I was in-the-know.

The difference between me and Sara Cwynar, I reflected, was that she was not buying candles to display in her home, to prove herself to be the sort of person who knew the best place to buy candles, but rather was buying them as an artist buys supplies: to use them for some other purpose. She was going to transform them, make them into something greater, something more *her* than *candle*. Whereas I would be, in buying a candle from candlestock.com, just a tourist in the life of art, the same way I feel people who buy saccharine journals, with pretty fabric covers festooned with a ribbon and gilt-edged pages, are tourists in the life of writing.

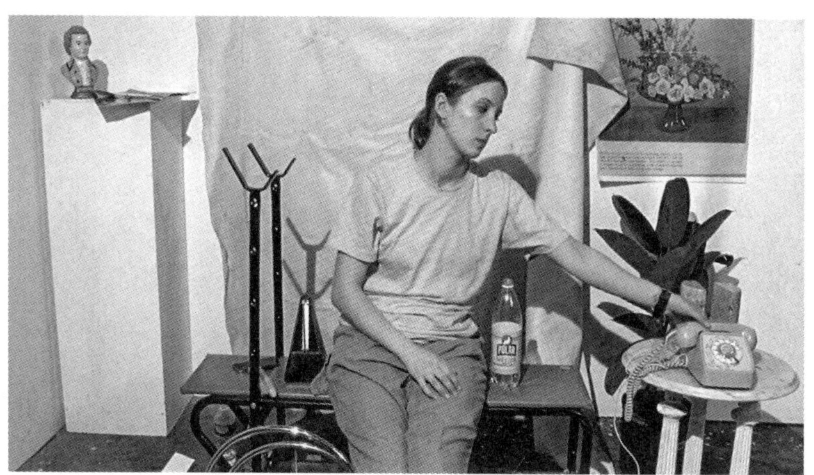

Sara Cwynar, "Rose Gold," 2017, video still. © Sarah Cwynar.

Sara was not buying candles at candlestock.com, a candle company based in Woodstock, New York, to pose before herself, or others, but because candlestock.com sold cheap drip candles in many colors. She would mess with them, break them down—not display them like status objects, conveying her grand leisure, the leisure of a woman who can source the best place to buy candles, a place that other women of leisure haven't discovered yet. This second person would be me. But who was I performing for? I am not on Instagram, showing off my life. Nobody comes to my house. I would be showing off my candles for me, and these candles would convince me that I had the intelligence, taste, and money, to source the most authentic sort of candles, thus proving myself to be superior to other women—proving this to myself for only a day or two—before the candles would become like everything else in my apartment: an extension of what I actually am, not what I hope to be.

All that time I was spending on candlestock.com I should have been spending on real research—reading interviews with Sara Cwynar, and looking more closely at her art than I was looking at the photographs of candles. How could my priorities have become so confused? Only because in some circles I have already proven myself to be enough of an intellectual to talk publicly about art, while I have still not yet proven to *anyone* that I am the sort of woman who knows how to furnish her house with the right sort of candles. All these thoughts were running through my mind as I was paging through candlestock.com. Then I shut down the website, having bought nothing, and I returned to my task, which was writing this lecture, which I had promised the gallery would be titled:

Should Artists Shop or Stop Shopping?

What can you do with no time and no money? asks the narrator in Sara Cwynar's video, *Soft Film*. Who is this person who has no time and no money?

The artist has time, but no money. The consumer has money, but no time.

To create her art, Sara Cwynar spends money like a consumer: she shops on eBay, she goes to dollar stores, she collects, she builds up her collection. Like the most distracted hoarder, she throws all of what she collects onto her floor in piles. There is some organization to her cataloging system, but not much. Or as she told *Interview* magazine, "There *is* an organizing principle! But it's just not very articulate, nor very good." To build her work, she "shops" from her floor, from the items she has collected because they appealed to her on a deep level—they stirred something in her person. Take the old velvet jewelry boxes she buys from eBay, with colors that have faded over time. They have changed more through time than the jewelry they once held. These boxes aren't supposed to be the focus of our attention: it's the jewelry that's supposed to be. But Cwynar wants the boxes. She is not a consumer with money but no time. She is an artist, with time but no money. The jewelry costs ten thousand dollars. The boxes cost ten.

So she has a bit of money, but more than that, she has time. She has time to buy things on eBay. And she has time to figure out what she wants and needs to buy. She has time to sift, to be led by her aesthetic sense, and her intelligence, and her vague premonition of what she will wind up making.

The non-artist consumer, who has money, but no time, buys what they are told to buy, or what they see other people buying, or what they imagine are the best things to buy. They do not buy according to some finely-chiseled inner compass, the way that Sara buys, or the way that a writer chooses her words.

Most of us buy to project something about ourselves to the world of people who witness us, or to tell ourselves that we are the sort of people we want to be. But Sara's time-rich consumer activity is different. It is different because the things she buys never seem expensive: a postcard with the Twin Towers on it; dishwashing gloves just the right color of red. They are never expensive because *she* is the only one who wants them. Things that are expensive are the things we all want. If we all had the time to want what *we in particular* want—to figure out what those wants might be, then spend our time finding them in stores or online—we would cut down our discretionary spending by so much.... But we have other things to do. We are not artists. Being not-artists, we buy what others buy, and spend so much more than we should.

Whenever something costs a lot, it's because everyone wants it. The reason you want it is because everyone wants it. And you want it *because* it costs a lot—you want it *more* because it costs a lot—because its costing a lot is a sign that it is wanted by many people. The fact that you can afford it and others cannot makes you feel like you are part of an elite circle that not only wants it (like everyone does) but can afford it (like only some).

To turn yourself into an artist, stop buying things that cost a lot. Buy the things that other people *don't* want—that only *you* want, because it's the right shade of green.

"The soft texture gets me here," the narrator of her video says, while her hands fondle the jewelry boxes. "Gets me here" means "gets me to the place of having bought these boxes." *The soft texture gets me here.* But *here* also means something more, for buying these boxes *has* got her *here*—to the place of standing in front of a camera in her studio, holding many old and faded jewelry boxes—*here* is the place in her process where she finds herself fondling the boxes, opening them, letting jewelry fall onto the floor out of them—the soft texture gets her *here*, to this very moment in her art-making.

I cannot say of any consumer product I have bought that it "gets me here," if *here* is someplace new, different from the old one. For me, a consumer, it is the reverse: buying keeps me in one place—the same place I was in when I bought the thing. I can only get to a new place if I *stop* buying—stop shopping on Amazon—stop succumbing to whatever material needs seem to emerge in the day. Buying *keeps* me here, in a certain state, a state of waiting (for the thing to arrive), a state of limbo (between my life as it is now, and the life I imagine I will live once I have it), a state of unreality, of wishful thinking, of magical thinking (that my life will be different once it arrives), a state of disappointment (when the thing I bought is absorbed into my life like everything else, and does not distinguish itself as new), a state of need (to buy the next thing that will lift me out of this here.) But what is this place I am in, and trying to escape? What is this *here*, but *shopping*? My home, and the computer on which I write, and the phone in my pocket, everything around me—has become a shopping mall. I am here in a shopping mall and I can't get out. I can only get out if I stop buying things.

I can only get out if I buy in the way of an artist—if I buy like Sara Cwynar.

■

The narrator in her video says, "I can't sleep so I comb eBay. Of course I can't sleep. There is too much to look at." I am not kept up at night, like Sara Cwynar is, by all there is to look at on eBay. I'm kept up at night by my greed—I'm kept up by the idea that these things on eBay *could be mine*.

■

Shopping is a form of creativity. When I am writing well, I feel no need for shopping. The times in my life I have shopped a lot, it is because I have not been writing.

Shopping is selecting. Writing is selecting.

Shopping is choosing the best thing. Writing is choosing the best thing (the best thing to write about, and the best way of writing it).

Shopping is articulating oneself through one's choices. Writing is articulating oneself through one's choices—choices made while writing.

If I tell myself I must not shop, I feel a deprivation and a fear. But if I actually *do not* shop, I feel self-contained and free. If I don't write, I feel deprivation and deadness.

Shopping sucks the creative energy out of my body—energy which could be put into writing—which I have instead put into shopping. Shopping makes me lose money. Writing earns me money. Writing gives me a feeling of satisfaction after having done it. Shopping gives me a feeling of nervous tension, anxiety, excitement and dread. When I have written on my computer, I have my riches there in front of me. When I have shopped online, the riches take days or weeks to come, and when they arrive, they no longer feel like riches. They are never all I hoped they would be. They are objects. They are not hopes. They are not wishes. They are not dreams. Writing—have been written—remains a hope, a dream, a wish. Why don't I write when I feel like shopping? For Sara Cwynar, shopping is necessary to make her art. It is not necessary for me. She has made shopping necessary for herself. She has made it something else.

When she shops for postcards, candles, and industrial tape, does she feel the way I do when I write, or does she feel the way I do when I shop? Or does she feel some other third thing?

What would it feel like to be like Sara Cwynar; to every day buy a postcard of the Twin Towers on eBay?

I buy a spiralizer, running shoes, vitamins, books, a pregnancy test, white t-shirts, light bulbs, an iPhone case, a milk frother, batteries. I do all my shopping on my computer. I do all my writing on my computer. Sometimes I shop from my gold-tone iPhone.

"As soon as you buy something, you lose the power to buy something," says the narrator in her video. Does this mean you lose the power to buy something because you've spent the money you'd need in order to buy the next thing? *As soon as you buy something, you lose the power to buy something.* I think the statement is more philosophical than that: as soon as you have the thing, you have lost *the power to buy* the thing. You cannot buy what you already have. It is the power to buy it that feels intoxicating. The thing—arriving as it does in the mail—is no longer (once you hold it in your hands) throbbing with your power to buy it, like you were throbbing when you added it to your cart. It is now inert with being owned.

■

"Objects are shocking because they stand in our way," the narrator of Sara Cwynar's video says. This may be true of some objects, but consumer objects are not, for the most part, shocking. They do not stand in our way. They are inevitable because they are put in our way, and when they arrive, their inevitability is all there is. *That's all right,* we quietly think, after we unpack the item and grasp it in its inevitable banality. *This is not a structural problem. It's that I have not yet bought the right thing.*

■

The narrator in Sara's video says, *The way that the things that were the most stylish are the ones to warp the most quickly.*

A consumer like me wants the things that are most stylish, and which consequently warp the most quickly.

The artist who buys for her own reasons and for her own pleasure, makes art out of the things she buys. They are transformed into her art, and art is the opposite of a most stylish thing that warps most quickly. Good art is most stylish and it never warps. Or it is unstylish when it first comes into the world, but it never warps the way fashion warps. The world warps to accept it.

Art holds within it the moment in culture in which it was produced—it preserves that cultural moment with all its contradictions and flux, so we can look at art, and understand the time it was produced in. Good art doesn't warp, grow gaudy or kitschy with age. Bad art warps. It grows as gaudy and kitschy as an ad in a magazine, or as a jewelry box on eBay. Bad art is like a stylish consumer product. Why does it warp? Why does it look so desirable one moment, then so awful the next, while good art is stable, and sits as itself, forever, in a culture which is ever warping?

In her video, she asks, "How do things become a glitch instead of an intention?" A glitch is what warps. An intention never does. A glitch is buying something impulsively on the internet. By the time it arrives, it has warped.

■

A sentence from Sara's film:

... an impulse to buy because this object truly is one-of-a-kind ...

A sentence from Sara's film:

... because it cannot be consumed, only contemplated ...

A sentence from Sara's film:

... pursue play ... that's what I'm going to do ...

A sentence from Sara's film:

... two thousand yards, one dollar fifty ...

A sentence from Sara's film:

... look at one thing at a time—just look, slowly, as if coming in from the side ...

A sentence from Sara's film:

Is the rose gold iPhone a totem? Does it signify an order? Maybe you won't even remember it at all.

A sentence from Sara's film:

Rose gold doesn't need to be anything at all—just an idea in the air; something to look forward to ...

■

I was corresponding with the poet Dorothea Lasky a few weeks ago. She teaches at Columbia University. She wrote me,

> My friend, Lucie Brock-Broido, passed away a few days ago. There are so many things to do because this just happened, but I feel I am too upset to do any of them, because I miss Lucie so much and am in this horrible nightmare state of shock where I am hoping I am *imagining* her gone and that I can just pick up the phone and call her. Then yesterday at 4:30 p.m. I taught my thesis class, where the students are making poetry books, and then went into Lucie's office and took pictures, trying to preserve and process *how she left her things*. She was a collector of things, as I am, and I knew everything was particularly placed. How things were placed by her is something I wanted to preserve.

I was struck by the idea that she wanted to preserve the *way* that Lucie placed things—that she felt this said something about Lucie, something that could not be said in another way, and so Dorothea felt she had to go in and photograph Lucie's office. It wasn't the *things* she collected that Dorothea was interested in—although she called Lucie "a collector of things," but rather she was interested in preserving "how she *left her things*."

A few emails later, Dorothea sent me a photograph of a corner of her own room at home. It seemed to be a white desk, with objects she had collected all arranged in a seemingly meaningful way: there were perhaps a hundred objects in the photograph: buttons, dolls, stickers, animal figurines, salt and pepper shakers, fortunes from fortune cookies, crayons, a mug, a tear-shaped mirror which dominated the desk, a tiny ship with sails. (As Sara's video says, *It is inevitably oneself that one collects*, and I felt this when I witnessed Dorothea's collection, as if seeing her in her nakedness.) Clearly every object in Dorothea's photo had been thoughtfully acquired, and purposefully kept, and deliberately placed in some arrangement with the other ones. I told her it looked like a shrine. But while this shrine was just for herself, and ugly in some way—like the desk of a teenage girl, cluttered with objects of personal meaning that could mean nothing to anyone else—Cwynar's arrangements of objects become works of art and beauty. Her arrangement is not just for herself—it is for us.

■

There is a world of objects collaged together which make up Sara Cwynar's flower still lives—buttons, candles, fake apples, shoelaces, light bulbs, books, straws, billiard balls, spools of thread, markers, paint brushes, toys—but the personal meaning they had for her (if they ever had personal meaning for her) has been stripped out of them. They seem meaningful only for their shape and color. They are at once what they originally were (those plastic gloves were made for washing dishes) and, in their new arrangement, have lost their original meaning (they're the right shape and color for that space). One's eye is constantly flickering between knowing the object, in all its banality, and losing a grip on its original purpose in favor of its current purpose: to be a thing of shape and color in a Sara Cwynar picture, to have an aesthetic relationship to the other objects there.

One thing we know about consumer objects is that they are supposed to lose their meaning—to flicker, let's say—only in the way the seller wants them to flicker. The sneaker can flicker between being something you put on your feet and something that raises your status in the world, but the flickering ought to stop there. The sneaker is not meant to flicker between being a status object and a flower vase. It is not meant to flicker between being a shoe and something else that's red. Of course once you've bought it, it will flicker between so many meanings: the meaning of when you wore it, or what your best friend said about it. The seller can't help that. But until it is bought, the meanings it is meant to flicker among are incredibly policed—and the more expensive it is, the more highly policed.

The meaning of a rose gold iPhone is supposed to flicker between ideas of luxury and status and newness—of a glossy future currently being born—but not flicker anywhere close to the idea of the puke green and bright orange that were once as desirable as rose gold is now. No one is policing the meaning of the things Sara buys to populate her videos—the old tape cassette, the discontinued spool of thread—because they cost two dollars, used.

■

At first, in the video *Rose Gold*, we get the sense that Sara has dodged beyond the clutches of the rose gold iPhone—the grip of its terrible beauty. She is thinking about what *rose gold* means, but this is an intellectual or aesthetic exercise. And then the words come: *I love the rose gold iPhone.*

She is as overcome by lust and desire for it as we all are. In the moment of her saying that, it has become for her what it is for everyone. In the next sentence, she calls it *a magical object*: "Old divisions between people and things are confused in this magical object."

The *thing* of this sentence is the iPhone, and the *people* in the sentence is our desire for it. The thing and the desire for the thing are confused. It's impossible to think about the thing—the iPhone—without thinking confusedly of the desire for it.

"Rose gold is flattering to most skin tones," her narrator continues, as if to apply scientific reasoning on why it's so desirable for so many, these phones we hold up against our faces. *Flattering to most skin tones!* That is not the reason we want the rose gold iPhone!

Now her narrator interjects, "Who is the voice of authority here, and who is this object actually for?" The voice of authority is clearly Apple, or whoever does their marketing, while *who is this object actually for?* It is not *for* anyone except for Apple. It is not for us, us sorry suckers, who could do without the rose gold iPhone. It is exclusively for its money-maker.

The video ends, "Is the rose gold iPhone a totem? Does it signify an order? Maybe you won't even remember it at all."

■

A few years ago, I edited a book called *Women in Clothes*. It was collaged together from the responses of 639 women from around the world to a survey my co-editors and I had put together about why women wear what they wear. Just like Sara Cwynar's work, the book, in part, dealt with the question of shopping—of collecting and displaying on your body—of what you chose to take from the world of objects, of which goods certain women find desirable, and why, and how they choose to arrange them—not on the studio floor, but the body. Many people answered our questions about shopping in ways you might imagine: most women seemed to know what they liked, and *why* they liked what they liked, and it all felt very personal, and very expressive of their lives and histories and likes and families and phobias and desires. If there was one thing that underscored the answers, it was that a woman's choices were meant—she knew—to do one thing above all else: reflect her individuality.

One of most divergent answers to the survey came in the form of a pamphlet or manifesto by my friend, the visual artist Margaux Williamson. It was a 24-point treatise, and it is a good example of how an artist chooses from the world of things, versus how a consumer chooses. The way that Margaux suggests we choose our clothes is a very close corollary to the way that Sara Cwynar models choosing from the miles of stuff listed on eBay.

Here are some points from her piece, a manifesto titled *How to Dress in Our New World*:

> *We used to dress to show the real us, or the other us, or of course to stay warm or without shame; to show our sex, our carelessness, our professionalism, our nihilism, our money; to be camouflage, a glossy magazine, a protest sign. But now we see—this old game is only a game of playing matchy matchy with our souls.*
>
> *The new game is to be misunderstood. And the new challenge is learning how to be misunderstood.*
>
> *Being misunderstood makes everything easier. It makes clothing acquisition less time-consuming. The contemporary situation is taking up plenty of your time, no time to waste.... We must find new ways to acquire clothing, new ways to show we are both of the sky and of the earth.*
>
> *So now if you find a T-shirt on the street and it is 100% cotton, maybe it is time to put it on. That is a great find, to find cotton*

on the street, so far away from the fields. And though it probably advertises a bad system that you don't believe in, everyone knows from your face what's in your heart. And besides, our personal investigations are as valuable as our speeches. See what it is like to match your face with the bad system …

If a kindly older woman gives you a coat that makes you look like you're on the wrong side of the money wars, wear that coat to your comrade or nemesis' dinner party. If we can't practice our beliefs and our empathy and our experiments over dinner, what is the point of dinner.

It might seem like, in the new world, clothes are nowhere to be found, but they are everywhere. In the desert, at the funeral home, in the garbage. There will never not be enough clothes. We made so many. Galaxies of factories were born in the name of individuality. Our person to clothing ratio spiraled out of control and the resulting great piles of clothes made more visible the meaninglessness of our individual lives on earth … Now, we must remember, the less effort we spend before that pile of production, the more meaning. It is not about finding the perfect you in that garbage heap, it is about economical movement and effort—what we can find here, at our feet—since you are very much you, and anything else is a juxtaposition, a gift.

So now, if you easily come across a dress that fits you like a glove, but makes you look like a stranger, remember, this is a fortune-telling game of meaning and ease—we must turn in the direction of what fits …

What we love now are worn things, things that have made it through experiences with what appear to be travel scars and thick skin …

Wash but do not make alterations. … Make no adjustments beyond what scissors can do. If the shirt is too big, you will look young and poor. If the shirt is too small, you will look big and strong. If the shirt is much too small, leave it on the street for a smaller hunter.

It's like the voice in Sara's video says: "Why would you make anything new … when there is so much already?"

■

I look at Etsy for the second time in an hour. I want everything I see on it! I like the feeling of wanting, and I hate the feeling of wanting. How can I be an artist on Etsy, instead of a consumer? What rules can I make for myself, when I'm browsing or shopping on the internet, that will turn me from a consumer into an artist? That will make me not go broke?

I imagine the rules Sara Cwynar has for herself as the same rules Margaux has:

Don't buy anything over twenty dollars.
Don't buy anything new.
Don't buy anything that you don't plan to combine with something else, or change or alter in some small way.
Don't buy something that doesn't make sense with everything you already have. It should match or contrast with it all, in some way.
Don't buy anything over fifteen dollars.
Don't buy anything over ten dollars.
Don't buy anything over five dollars.
Don't buy anything over two.

■

When I follow these rules online, I find a world of stuff that looks like Margaux's closet, and that looks like the objects in Sara Cwynar's video.

■

Things that are already gone the same moment that they arrive, her narrator warns…

Which is the perfect definition of everything I order over the internet. They are gone the moment they arrive.

How can I remind myself, when I'm browsing online, that I don't want anything once it comes? I want the looking, the choosing—the creativity involved in picking—the feeling of having *caught it,* before anyone else does—the looking forward to it arriving, and the great feeling of power of being able to buy. I want everything *except* the object, which sticks its tongue out at me as I pull it from the box.

I read a book by a woman who wrote a blog about how she was not going to buy anything for an entire year. She was a smart woman, an Upper East Side mom. She was a television writer, and quite rich. She began with such bravado and certainty. And she lasted all of three months. She failed in front of everyone. She pretended her failure was no big deal.

Who among us will crack the code, and tell it to all the others? Tell the others how to have the *feeling* of consuming without buying anything?

■

Sara Cwynar looks for what there is to buy, but the meanings of the objects for sale—their meanings are entirely hers. The things she acquires gain value only because she picked them. She bought them, she arranged them, side-by-side with other things. She filmed them and showed them to us. She put them in a beautiful frame, the beautiful frame of her videos.

If any of the things she shows in her videos came to my house instead, they would not give me the same feeling that they give me there in her videos. They are beautiful because they are *hers*, and not mine. Because she is beautiful, and I am not. Because her life is beautiful, and mine is not. This is what it all comes down to. Whenever anything becomes mine, it becomes like me. And what is me but this chaos, this meaninglessness, this sloppiness and imperfection. She might be all those things for herself, too, but because she has put herself into her beautiful art, she is not that for *me*. She is like her beautiful art: finished, finite, ordered, edited, shot, selected, meaningful—and everything she touches in those videos has meaning and orderliness, too.

■

Her films are delicious. I want my life to be the color of her films, and for my days to be arranged by the same hands that move the face on her clock to 8:20. I want her face to be my face, and for her boyfriend to have once been mine. I want the bed I am lying in to be her bed, which is tinted red by a red gel over the lights. I want to buy little jewelry boxes, too, and to not be able to sleep from looking sideways at every page on eBay. I want to wear her perfect clothes, that are baggy and interesting colors, and don't look like they cost much. I want her pretty face and big eyes, and her long hair and her sneakers. I want even the sneakers that she wears in the video that she says she does not like. I want to have a studio with a floor full of things that I arrange, and to work every day with my hands, arranging. I want to make the videos she made, and to smile, like she does, at the man behind the camera while lying in a bed. I want all of that as much as I want whatever it is I bought on eBay, or Amazon, or Etsy, today or the day before yesterday.

I can't have her things, her face, her life. But I can have it, too. I can look at her videos all I want. But I don't want to look at them! I want to eat them. I don't even want to eat them—I want her videos to be my life. I know it's no more her life, those seven-minute videos, than "partying on a back deck in the summer with bikini-clad women and muscly men" is the life of any of the actors in the beer ad. Yet this has nothing to do with the actors in a beer ad, because *she made it.* She made those videos! So even if it's not her external life, it *is* her *internal* life. If I watched her videos a hundred times, perhaps I could make her world mine. That would be a way of eating it. And yet I know I won't. I won't watch her videos a hundred times. I want her world to be mine much *more easily* than that. I want her world to be mine by putting it in a cart on the internet, and buying it, and having it arrive at my door, and unpacking it, and knowing it's mine and no one else's. All the things of the world I want—I am too impatient to slowly imbibe them. I want to purchase them and have them in my home, and go to bed and be done. The only way to imbibe art, to imbibe anything, is—as the voice in her video said, to *look at one thing at a time—just look, slowly, as if coming in from the side...*

Am I still capable of looking slowly, as if coming in from the side? Or have I ruined myself? Can I now only buy?

■

How can I make my stuff meaningful enough for myself that I never have to buy anything anymore? Must I arrange it all better in my house, the way she arranges things in front of the camera, moving them around? Yes. I won't buy anything anymore. I'll just move what I have, around. I'll jump right to that phase of the artistic process: not the ordering from eBay phase of Sara's artistic process, or my own sickly consumerism—but the organizing on the ground phase of the artistic process. Proceed as though you have all the things. You probably *do* have all the things. And you have thrown so many things out!

■

I'd really never thought before of rearranging the things I have—or considered that an artist edits, arranges and puts things in the right place, a place that gives them beauty and meaning. When something comes to my doorstep, it is just a thing, like when words fall onto my page, they are just words, fallen onto whiteness. It is the arrangement and placement and all of the editing that charges them with meaning: it is the *working* with the words that make them mine. So might it be with the things that come to me in the mail, that I ordered mindlessly on eBay: by working with them, arranging them, forever and for their lifespans, putting them here, moving them there, tending to them, combining them—it might be doing *this* that will change them from the inert thing that arrives at my door, which I always feel a kind of disappointment at receiving, into something charged, more like art, charged with my being, with meaning and purpose and feeling. That would finally make them mine, and would endow them with something greater than the banality of possession.

Then I *will* keep my things in constant motion, like Sara does in her videos, always moving objects around, first here, then there, so they are constantly changing meaning, their relationships always changing. When she removes something from a scene, it is like she is swiping it from her phone; removing one object, or placing it somewhere new. Swiping is creating, it's a kind of magic, it makes things appear and disappear. But swipe *not* just to put something in your cart. The swiping must continue once the object is yours. The ever-swiping makes you an artist. The swiping gives it meaning.

■

Sara Cwynar's narrator says, "My skin falls but rose gold doesn't change."

Rose gold is an ideal, perfection. Rose gold is nothing. It is just two words. It cannot decay or change.

Rose gold cannot be what she loves. The things she likes to collect are jewelry boxes that fade, and are beautiful for their fading. They represent an eternal color: the fading color of time. What is the color of time? It is the color of fading. It colors every other color.

We should see the things we own as having more and more value, as their color mixes with the color of time, as the things we own *become* time. Part object, and part time.

■

In *Rose Gold* we see all these fingers, swiping, observed from behind a glass, these little gestures, so delicate, so small. The narrator says of life now—the life we live on our iPhones: *Reality is touched not with direct confidence but with fingertips that are immediately withdrawn.* That is how we go at consuming—we are tentative and we are scared. We consume not with direct confidence, but with fingertips that are immediately withdrawn. She moves the objects in her videos, always moving them about. She makes art *not with direct confidence, but with fingertips that are immediately withdrawn.* The more I write this phrase, the more beautiful it becomes. Is that what life is—not a path proceeded along with direct confidence, but with fingertips that are immediately withdrawn? Is that how we love now? Not with direct confidence, but with fingertips that are immediately withdrawn?

■

I emailed Dorothea Lasky, saying that although I buy things for my home, for my body, I actually don't collect things, the way she does—the way her shrine revealed. I buy things but I *also* throw things out, suddenly and with great need. That is my great compulsion. I take great pleasuring in throwing things out. In throwing out, suddenly, all the things I have bought. Is it because they disgust me? Do they threaten to hold me down, so that I can no longer shift and move, like the objects on the floor of Sara Cwynar's studio? There are so many clothing items, objects I look back on, and wonder why I threw them out. I feel ashamed because my reason was so spontaneous and emotional: it was in my house and, irritated one day, I felt it *must* be gone.

I had told Dorothea that the photograph of her desk seemed like an altar or a shrine. She said she *does* think of her collection as a shrine. She wrote, "The accumulation of these things in a particular placement is a type of prayer that to me resists the idea that there is a way to do it. Like *oh yellow cup, of course put that in the cupboard, duh!* But it's like, NO, I want to put it HERE."

I read that and thought, *I have no shrine. I have no type of prayer. I buy compulsively and I throw out like a bulimic—I'm a bulimic with my things.*

She said, "I think your instinct to not have things, to throw them out, feels the same as my compulsion to make my shrines. There is a severe need in both instincts to control what we do—and not have it be because some other force thought it should be some way. Maybe this is about being an artist, too. It's about, my life's purpose is to do *this* to things. And things can be words. I mean, of course they are."

Katie Kitamura

Katie Kitamura is a Japanese American critic and novelist, whose writing practice is grounded in professional and critical training (she completed a PhD on the aesthetics of vulgarity in the modern novel), and whose first book was *Japanese for Travellers* (2006): a nonfiction exploration of belonging, progress, and decay that questioned ideas of insider and outsider status. Since then, she has published three novels—*The Longshot* (2009), *Gone to the Forest* (2013), *A Separation* (2017)—a range of art criticism for magazines like *Frieze* and *Contemporary*, alongside more journalistic pieces for the *Guardian* and the *New York Times*. Her critical attention tends to focus on different techniques for building narrative, building parallels between different media. She has written about how, in the field of history, "digital culture . . . aids and abets" a process of "fragmentation," before contemplating how it would be "possible to harness some of that strangeness and that energy." In this essay, she draws similarly unexpected parallels with video installation art, explaining that "the feeling I had, the first time I saw *Nostalgia*, was that Omer Fast was evidently one of the best fiction writers working today." Attuned to, but wary of, David Shields's argument in *Reality Hunger* (2009), Kitamura nuances that "reality itself, on the other hand, is an unstable and contingent field, as likely to be contaminated by fiction as the other way around."

The Hunger

Omer Fast's three-part video installation *Nostalgia* (2009) begins modestly, with what appears to be documentary footage of a white man in a wood, wearing camouflage gear and setting a trap built out of a stick and string. The scene plays on a small flat screen, attached to the outside wall of the installation, and is accompanied by a voice-over recounting instructions for building a trap. Over the course of the installation, the work's screens grow larger and multiply, and the ostensible reality of this initial footage is pulled apart.

In the second part of *Nostalgia*, an interview between an African asylum seeker and a white filmmaker (possibly representing Fast, as played by an actor) runs on two facing screens, with the audience sandwiched in the middle of the exchange. The atmosphere between the two men—the approximate dimensions of the room on screen re-created in the physical space of the gallery—is tense, awkward. The politics of race and power constantly threaten to erupt, as the filmmaker character considers employing the asylum seeker for a project about Africa. Gradually, snippets of dialogue from the documentary footage playing outside the gallery appear in the interview footage, until we hear the asylum seeker recounting instructions for setting a trap—the first part's voice-over now categorized as pilfered and artificially grafted onto the documentary image, whose authenticity is thus called into question.

The third part of *Nostalgia* leaps wholeheartedly into the world of fiction. An extended piece of speculative invention, this final section is lushly shot in 16mm and adopts a 1970s palette. It also has its foundation in the complex world of racial politics established in the first two parts, imagining an inverted world in which white refugees attempt to illegally enter a democratic African nation whose borders are tightly patrolled, by way of a series of underground tunnels.

In this gradual slide from documentary into fiction over three parts, the work's fictional apparatuses are elaborated and rendered visible. As a whole, *Nostalgia* most obviously owes a debt to various genres of film, from documentary to science fiction. However, the feeling I had, the first time I saw *Nostalgia*, was that Omer Fast was evidently one of the best fiction writers working today.

■

In 2010, David Shields published his book *Reality Hunger*, which was rapidly embraced as a call to action aimed at fiction writers in particular. In large part a collation of quotations from diverse sources—novelists and critics, with a handful of artists and filmmakers thrown in—the short book argues that the present moment is marked by a powerful longing for the real. Shields identifies "reality hunger" in artistic production across mediums and genres, from reality television to films such as *Borat* (2006): "An artistic moment, albeit an organic and as-yet-unstated one, is forming. What are its key components? A deliberate unartiness: 'raw' material, seemingly unprocessed, unfiltered, uncensored and unprofessional."

In his manifesto—which offers self-described guidelines for authorship—Shields posits reality as an open-source network of sorts, from which the frisson of "the real" can be endlessly pilfered. The problem is that Shields is largely describing a reality effect, a set of signifiers that are instantly recognizable—in the way that a hand-held camera denotes authenticity, or graininess indicates the "unprocessed" and "unfiltered." Reality itself, on the other hand, is an unstable and contingent field, as likely to be contaminated by fiction as the other way around.

The work of artists such as Fast suggests an alternative approach, an almost perfect inversion of Shields's manifesto. Rather than injecting reality into fiction, fiction can be used to perceive the contours of what we describe as reality, to rearticulate the frame through which we perceive the terrain of fact.

The deployment of fiction against the landscape of reality is particularly potent in relation to politics—a realm that is curiously and problematically absent from *Reality Hunger*—and forms the basis for several artists working in film and video today, including Eric Baudelaire, Anja Kirschner and David Panos, Roee Rosen and Hito Steyerl. Here, fiction in its most recognizable forms allows artists to explore the structure of political fictions. Steyerl's *November* (2004), for example, combines the language of home video and news footage with

B-movies to tell the story of Steyerl's long-time friend, Andrea Wolf, who joined the Kurdish liberation movement, and was killed in 1998. The work moves backward and forward in time, cutting between a home video featuring Steyerl and Wolf as teenagers, martial-arts movies and documentary—fragments that are tied together with a voice-over drawn from the artist's own memories of Wolf. Steyerl's work—in which she often features—is a good example of how the exploitation of a certain reality effect (in this case, documentary footage and personal recollection of a close friend who has since died) is cut with self-conscious fictional devices. The contingent nature of what we experience as reality, particularly in the political realm, is made visible through the openly declared artifice of fiction.

What is common to these artists is the notion that reality—particularly difficult realities, of political and personal trauma—can sometimes be accessed only through fiction. Perhaps the most salient recent example of this is Joshua Oppenheimer's feature-length documentary *The Act of Killing* (2012). The film focuses on members of the Indonesian death squads that killed more than a million civilians following the military coup in 1965. The accounts of these men—who have never been prosecuted for their crimes—are augmented by staged scenes utilizing various film genres, from musicals to Westerns. The men conceive, write and star in the scenarios and, in this way, the documentary tells the story of their crimes.

■

Like Fast's *Nostalgia*, Anja Kirschner and David Panos's *Polly II* (2006) frames present-day politics of capital and gentrification through the structure of science fiction. Set in a future London, the film creates a flood zone located in the ruins of east London. In staging this world on screen, Kirschner and Panos employ deliberately shoddy post-production techniques: the flood water imperfectly dropped into the image, the flames of a fire incorrectly scaled, the special effects falling apart at the seams.

The result is a moving image that feels like collage. It could be categorized as the intrusion of reality—the edit suite apparent in every image breaks up the fiction of the narrative. But it feels less like a manifestation of "reality" and more like the intrusion of what is termed the Lacanian "Real"—an eruption into the apparently smooth

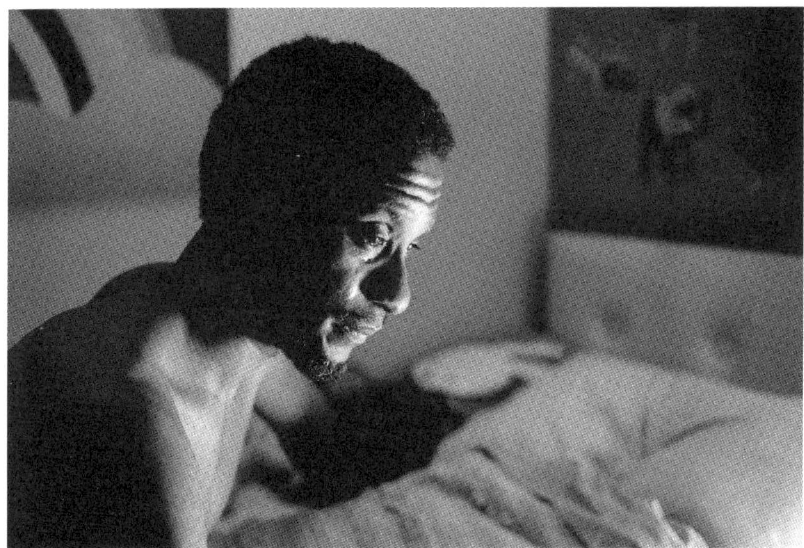

Omer Fast, "Nostalgia," 2009, video still. © Omer Fast.

and consistent surface of our world, a traumatic reminder of the contingent nature of our reality. In *Polly II*, it's not that reality interrupts a fiction, it's rather that we see reality lose its texture altogether.

Fast's post-production technique—specifically his editing—similarly effects a traumatic intrusion of the Real. His two-channel video installation *Godville* (2005) takes as its primary source material interviews with "interpreters" working at the living-history museum of Colonial Williamsburg in Virginia. From these interviews, Fast selects individual words and phrases, carving out his own text from a pre-existing block of language. The result is twofold. On one side of a suspended screen, the composite voice-over that Fast has edited together accompanies footage shot around the town of Williamsburg. The effect is seamless, notwithstanding the disjunction between the content of the voice-over and the accompanying images. On the other side, the radically edited footage of the interviews—the original images that accompany the composite audio—is screened.

Among other things, Fast plays with the markers of documentary, interview and testimony. But what's most striking is the unnatural quality of the edited interview footage. The bodies of the interview subjects twitch and leap on the screen according to the rapid and irregular cuts; the camera remains fixed on a body in extremis. The interpreters are recorded in locker rooms as they prepare for work. They put on their costumes, colonial-period dresses and suits, but are placed against the backdrop of a modern-day interior. That's an inclusion of a reality that breaks the fiction of the re-enactment. But in the spasm-ridden figures of his edited subjects, Fast pushes that rupture further, into a dimension of the Real instead of mere reality, into the uncanny rather than the authentic. That's what makes the work so compelling. Fast, or indeed Kirschner and Panos, aren't exposing the material fictions of their work out of any hunger for "reality"—in too many cases a simple byword for authenticity of personal experience (hence Shields's interest in confessional narrative). Rather, they're drawing out a stranger and more compelling dimension that lies concealed in fiction. That element constantly threatens to expose itself, and is finally what gives fiction—from the cinematic or literary to the broader realm of narration and invention—its tension. "Reality," as such, is merely a stop on the way.

Chris Kraus

Chris Kraus is an art critic, video-art maker, editor at experimental publisher Semiotext(e), and the author of four semiautobiographical novels. Alongside her fiction, Kraus has published a number of books of essays and a biography of the experimental writer Kathy Acker; the two strands of Kraus's writing converge in their shared subject matter: the place (and potential) of the female artmaker (also the subject of her *Native Agents* series at Semiotext(e)) and the larger question of the role of art in contemporary culture. It is no coincidence that her 2018 book-length essay is simply titled *Where Art Belongs*. Reframed as a question, "Who gets to speak and why?" was the refrain of Kraus's polemical novel of the late 1990s: *I Love Dick*. Two decades later, the novel became a feminist talisman for the "woke" young (following its UK release in 2016, there wasn't a bus in Britain that didn't have a young woman holding its lurid green and pink cover). *I Love Dick* is driven forward by a woman who wants, but is failing, to be an artist, who wants to create art from love, and love from art. In the vein of her critical predecessors like Susan Sontag, Kraus is fascinated with the erotics of art—though in this essay, on LA's art scene in the early 2000s, Kraus meditates on a different kind of attraction: that of belonging to a community of artists, of finding a place outside of, or at least in parallel to, the commercial art world of global art centers like New York.

A Walk around the Neighborhood

"LA is not so much a city full of alternative spaces, but an alternative space in itself, a perpetual frontier, peripheral to the financial and museological center of the US artworld, New York, but still possessing a vitality that would be embarrassing to ignore. There are bursts of lexical enthusiasm for 'LA art' in the form of emotionally sincere and deliriously subjective marketing literatures, almost identical in their perspectives, appearing every five years or so, almost like clockwork," as the late New Zealand artist-turned-curator Giovanni Intra observed in an essay written for the *Circles.1* exhibition at ZKM.

Intra moved to LA in 1996 and rightly sensed the city's possibilities. As provincial as his native Auckland, LA was also as diverse and vibrant as New York or London. After putting in an obligatory three years at ArtCenter College of Design's graduate program, he cofounded China Art Objects, the renegade commercial gallery that spawned a micro-revolution when it opened in 1999. After its first year in business, new galleries opened in adjacent storefronts by the week. Until then, nearly all of LA's commercial galleries were located in upscale neighborhoods like Santa Monica and Brentwood, on the west side. Finally, the art scene was about to move to where the artists actually lived. China's instant success signaled downtown LA's first wave of gentrification—an "economic miracle" that had eluded developers for two decades.

"Of course we will take advantage of this in whichever way seems appropriate or possible at the time, but it's not exactly riding the jock of genius," Intra concluded in his essay about LA for ZKM Karlsruhe.

When I moved to LA from the East Village in 1995, I was amazed by the hegemony graduate art education held over the city's art world. LA was, after all, the second-largest city in the US. Routinely touted as the "first twenty-first-century city," it was, and remains, one of the great immigrant capitals of the world. Yet in the mid-1990s there was just one port of entry to the commercial gallery system, and that was attendance at one of three high-profile graduate programs. Usually, about a quarter of their graduates attained A- or B-list gallery representation upon leaving school. Alternative spaces had no credibility. Graduating with as much as $100,000 in debt, younger artists had to create salable work as soon as they could. Yet the very success of this narrow system changed it, in unpredictable ways. Thousands of talented artists flocked to attend school in LA, and they stayed. Artists have opened their own galleries, boutiques, and bars. The look is less uniform, and "success"—defined as the ability to keep making art—is now achieved here in numerous ways.

Writing for Susan Kandel's *Art/Text* magazine between 1998 and 2001, I studied the Los Angeles art world in an anthropological way. I liked a lot of the people I met and tried to keep an open mind. The artists I talked to for this book are all committed to pursuing original work on their own terms. Some, like Henry Taylor, are on the verge of international careers. Others, like Eugenia Butler, have continued working in ebbs of fame and obscurity across decades. I think they all have succeeded in channeling the possibility and freedom this city affords. Are they representative? Yes and no. As Walter Mosley, the author of more than a dozen philosophical-sleuth novels set in LA's notorious South Central "ghetto," observed, "My father said: 'Los Angeles already had a structure. As people came here, they brought another structure. As they came together, it made a city that was impossible to know.'"

Which is to say, there are many LAs.

■

Northeast Los Angeles, sometime in 2002: we're in a spacious California Craftsman bungalow, the Craftsman house everyone wants, as featured in architectural magazines. The house is discreetly set into the Mount Washington hillside, and we're being guided through it by Delia Brown's trancey, transcendent Steadicam. Five minutes, without traffic, from downtown, Mount Washington looks over the northeast LA neighborhood of Highland Park. With its green belt of Santa Monica Conservancy tracts and winding streets named after birds, Mount Washington used to be known as "the Brentwood of the ghetto." The writer Dalton Trumbo, blacklisted throughout most of the 1950s, holed up in a Mount Washington cabin to write *Spartacus*. Since then, the neighborhood has become much more upscale, home to attorneys, movie producers, City Council officials, and such artists as Shirley Tse and Jorge Pardo.

This particular Craftsman house is halfway up the hill, and we're at a gathering of friends on what seems to be a gentle Sunday afternoon. The camera floats around the party in one long, four-minute take. The party feels as if it could go on forever. It might still be going on now. Goapele, the exquisitely beautiful young Oakland-based R&B singer whose independently produced debut album recently hit *Billboard*'s top-100 chart, sits on one of the couches, gazing into her diary. A community activist since her teens, Goapele's name means "to move forward" in the South African language Setswana. She's wearing a light-as-air summer dress and lip-syncing the lyrics to her hit single "Closer":

I'm getting higher
Closer to my dream
Feel it in my sleep

The camera's getting closer too, but not too close: just enough to show the house and those who inhabit it on this afternoon: the multicolored angelfish in the aquarium, the stocky white guy and his girlfriend kissing in the hallway on a cushioned Mission bench. A tranced-out Bathsheba dances on an oriental carpet in the living room; she wears a purple jersey dress.

Sometime: it feels like I'll never go past here
Sometime: it feels like I'm stuck, forever,

sings Goapele, but if she's stuck, there are worse places than this to be. Here, suspended in this light, among the wood and glass and outdoor bougainvillea, a Black couple lean against the rail of a redwood balcony, deep in conversation. Two white girls walk down to the koi pond and leave their sandals on a ledge. Back in the living room, a gold-leafed Buddha gazes tranquilly at champagne mimosas on the table. A woman lying on the floor leafs through a magazine. Red wine and Tiffany lamps. Books everywhere, a guitar thrown casually on the sofa, framed works of art.

The day is mellow, smooth, but not without a little tension. Seen through the open kitchen doorway, a man and woman lean against the kitchen counters exchanging words. She frowns, she gestures with her hands. Challenged, he gazes at the floor, stiffens, and then pulls back. Still, the tension here is like the backbone of the lizard: there's just enough to give the afternoon some shape. Out on the deck, a white woman in a neo-psychedelic caftan blows bubbles from a wand and rocks her toddler gently to the beat.

Staged by the Los Angeles-born artist Delia Brown, the film, called *Pastorale* (2002), enacts a kind of paradise. The kind of multiracial paradise of informed, discreet consumption that LA could maybe be—a collective cumulative fantasy dreamed by millions, perfected by Steadicam, and shown, minus the dreary plots and dialogue, on afternoon TV. Writing in *The New York Times*, the reviewer Ken Johnson pointed out that *Pastorale* "would seem to mock the infantile complacency of people protected by unearned privilege." But when I saw it in San Francisco in 2004 in Ralph Rugoff's knockout *Baja to Vancouver* West Coast show, the first thing I thought was, "I want to live in this world, too."

Months later, when we meet for drinks at The Arsenal, a reconstructed dive bar in Santa Monica, Brown talks about the curious response to *Pastorale* that she initially received: "People who knew my work said *Pastorale* was a departure. They said: we don't see the cynicism, where's the irony? And I was like, yeah—that's true. Because I don't like to see my work in terms of irony, I like to move in and out. I never wanted to paint myself into this ironic corner. People talked about the song as music for boutiques and bubble baths, and this seemed so degrading. Maybe the piece got away from me in the process of making it, but originally I meant it as an ode to Goapele . . . she is an intensely strong soul, and to me 'Closer' was a very uplifting song, a contemporary spiritual."

Brown is a compact, energetic woman in her mid-thirties. Before attending UCLA she'd almost made a go of a career in rap, mentored by the manager of the illustrious Wu-Tang Clan. She's white. Given *Pastorale*'s graceful, effortless biracial casting (and the almost total absence of Black subjects in white, post-art school LA art), I'd just assumed that Brown was Black.

"I was feeling frustrated," she said, "by the way you're often bound, as a visual artist, to create a critical practice. I'm happy to have my work be critical, as much as possible. But I want to also feel the potential for making work that creates a transcendent experience for the viewer. So often with visual art you have to penetrate its conceptual strategies and its history to feel anything at all. Music is more giving to the receiver. So a part of this came out of a major envy of Goapele: here she was, ten years younger than me, with this extraordinary gift, and working in an art form that I'm jealous of."

Brown graduated from UCLA's MFA Studio Art program in 2000. She sees art as an opportunity to probe the triggers of desire and, in the process, make them come true. Her debut Show featured mother-daughter paintings of herself with her LA gallerist, Margo Leavin. "All artists," Brown explains, "have some sort of parent/child relation to their dealers. And Margo personified the kind of mother that I'd fantasized having in my teens: she was single, cultured, very glamorous. My parents are in the health-care field, so I always fantasized having a mom who smoked cigarettes and wore red Chanel lipstick and partied with her friends."

Critics saw the image differently. Was Brown a social climber, thrusting herself into the arms of this powerful art world woman? Well, yes and no. "When I was growing up, I had to buy all my clothes at JC Penney," Brown recalls. "My friend from Beverly Hills bought all of hers at Neiman Marcus. Her mom was single, and I imagined her with this fabulous lifestyle, smoking a joint in the evening. Margo embodied that to me."

Shades of resentment. I think that Brown's a bold and brilliant artist, playing with a fuller deck than most. Still, it's these differences, between JC Penney and Neiman Marcus, between opulent wealth and lower-middle class, that are most visible in LA.

> A vertiginous hump of residential bleakness ... a yawning blackness sprinkled here and there with streetlamps ... the air fraught with the howling of dogs, a regular keening that carries on half the night and sometimes all night ... myriad agitated semiferal dogs chained in myriad desolate dustridden yards choked with cinder blocks piled under flapping tarpaper ...

is how Gary Indiana described the neighborhood below Brown's paradisiacal hill in *Resentment*, his great 1997 LA book.

What struck many visitors about Los Angeles in the wake of the 1994 South Central riots was just how *nice* the ghetto looked, at least from outside. The same bougainvillea that twists around the redwood deck in *Pastorale* blooms in Watts outside tidy single-family brick and wood-frame homes. Watts, scene of the cataclysmic riots of the mid-'60s, and home of the Watts Towers, one of the most extraordinary constructions within American outsider art, embodies LA's wild contradictions. As Lynell George noted recently in the *Los Angeles Times*:

> on this short stretch of 107th street, small bungalows painted the cheerful pastels of Easter eggs sit behind flowerbeds bearing succulents; grandmothers chat across the fence in dancing Spanish; kids zip by on bikes. But just an echo away, a police cruiser has pulled up alongside a purring and primered sedan; a teenage boy missing one leg rolls by in a wheelchair; a weathered O.G. wheels by a block away, missing both.

I'm reminded of how Easy Rawlins, the protagonist of Walter Moseley's mystery *A Red Death*, describes his Watts house on 116th Street, circa 1954:

> I had a small house, but that made for a large front lawn. In recent years I had taken to gardening. I had daylilies and wild roses against the fence, and strawberries and potatoes in large rectangular plots at the center of the yard. There was a trellis that enclosed my porch, and I always had flowering vines growing there.... But what I loved most was my avocado tree. It was 40 feet high with leaves so thick and dark that it was always cool under its shade.... When things got really hard, I'd sit down there to watch the birds chase insects through the grass.

■

The artist Daniel Mendel-Black lives and works in a Figueroa Boulevard storefront down the hill in Highland Park, two miles south of Brown's *Pastorale*. It's very urban here, with a surviving pay phone in the street and a graffiti'd canvas awning outside a low-slung white stucco apartment building.

And in fact, the history of this genetic structure, with fluted deco-modern porticos slapped onto the roofline in a passing nod to architecture, encapsulates the history of the neighborhood. Originally a Mexican dancehall bar, it served later as a sweatshop until the garment industry moved south. When Mendel-Black moved in, he had to rip out vats of toxic chemicals left behind by a methamphetamine operation that had set up there for a while.

Across the street, the El Recreo Social Club stays open until four a.m., shuttling patrons back and forth to a nearby brothel. Mendel-Black's Russian neighbor deals in carpet remnants, vinyl tiles. With a Home Depot just three blocks away, his Color Carpet store does very little home improvement trade, but the owner's on the phone all day. The storefront Daniel occupies is cheap, and huge. Its plateglass windows looking out on Figueroa Boulevard are draped in rice paper, and everything inside is washed diffusely in pearlescent light. Books on Gilles de Rais and Jewish mysticism vie for space with horror comics on the artist's thrift-store couch.

Works in various stages of completion are scattered around the loft. There's a sheaf of gorgeous black and white ink drawings near the window: stalactites of spiderwebs melting in the dark. For the past two years Mendel-Black has pursued a heady mix of minimalist grids gone horribly—and biomorphically—wrong. His works—which take the form of paintings, sculptures, drawings—are like a gross-out ode to Agnes Martin. In *Diseased Love* (2004), organic tubes curl up into rectangles, white Squares light up darkened cubes like windows in an office building, and spray-painted circles radiate in whiteness from the center of melted Matisse-like forms. "The tissue of the brain and the intestine are identical," the artist notes.

The son of two artists based in Washington DC, Mendel-Black arrived in LA in 1994 to do an MFA at ArtCenter College of Design. In the early '90s he had worked briefly as a studio assistant to Peter Halley in New York. Before moving out to California, he moved back to DC and took a more regular job, as editorial assistant at *The Washington Post*. He chose ArtCenter because it seemed more intellectual. He studied mid-century artists such as Robert Ryman in depth and was impressed by how Ryman gleefully trashed the expressionist impulse by making paintings according to arithmetic formulae and mechanical means.

"When I came out here in 94," he told me, "it wasn't about being in the LA art scene. It was about going to school, where there was an environment based on working out certain issues in contemporary art—it was almost an intellectual merit system—but when I graduated it was a shock to find that in the LA artworld, that wasn't actually what was happening at all. I thought there'd be an openness and freedom, a large-scale experiment going on, but instead there was this kind of false professionalism, everybody acting as if there was all this money to be made."

Perhaps naively, Mendel-Black believed that these schools were preparing people for lives of artistic reflection rather than for commercial careers. "For years it was a very lonely activity to be an artist here, though that might seem strange, considering the schools are pumping out hundreds of kids a year. But really the schools produced a lot of artists who were made entirely reliant on institutional structures. I was shocked, given the paucity of what the commercial gallery system has to offer, that people started putting so much faith in these institutions. They lost sight of the fact that art should be based on whatever it was the artist wants to do."

"This produced a kind of sadness. It became clear that a lot of artists just wanted to get their seat on the bus as quickly as possible and not think about other things."

Stranded in the very un-minimal environment of Highland Park, Mendel-Black soon began working on his own projects, thinking about how to create alternative outlets for himself and his friends. In 1999 he started *Spring Journal*—the title an ironic nod to German romanticism, but also the much less ironic belief that it might be possible for artists to rely on one another and, in so doing, make a fresh start.

In subsequent issues the journal has published articles challenging contemporary art world nostalgia and attacking the romantic myth of the artist's or writer's unselfconscious, willed naiveté. Contributors have included such distinguished artists and writers as John Miller, Larry Rickles, André Butzer, Martin Prinzhorn and Benjamin Péret.

Spring Journal has attracted German collaborators who, like Mendel-Black and his friends, are prepared to challenge all received ideas. "The rebellion we inherited," Mendel-Black says of his generation, "wasn't Expressionism or Situationism like the Europeans. Our history is more based on an irrational suspicion of the inside world. What makes it so neurotic is its equally cynical Romanticism of the outside world—hi-tech, consumer culture, the desert landscape, etc. The Europeans equate American minimalism with a punk rock militancy towards visual culture. For me it is not the one over the other. It is the combination of these and other attitudes that by all accounts are supposed to ideologically oppose each other that can really open a discussion up again."

Recently, with some German friends, together with the LA-based sci-fi writer Mark von Schlegell and the Chinatown gallerist Joel Mesler, Mendel-Black produced Ten Thousand Fair Afflictions: The First Annual Extremist Conference at The Mountain, artist Jorge Pardo's upscale Chinatown art bar. Among the many high points of the event was André Butler's recital of fragments of writings by Jacques Lacan as a primal scream, accompanied by his friend, Professor Winkler, who played sugar-sweet acoustic pop songs on guitar.

■

A gray Saturday morning in late February, I'm sitting around the Pruess Press gallery with the gallery owner Joel Mesler, the writer Mark von Schlegell, and my friend Goody-B. Wiseman, an artist who's recently moved down here from San Francisco. It's still early here on Bernard Street in Chinatown, but by eleven we've all arrived.

The activities of Pruess Press revolve around a huge dual-etching lithography press that Mesler bought from an old print shop in the Valley. Used since the 1930s to print trade union pamphlets, supermarket flyers, and suburban newspapers, the press is presently deployed in cranking out commemorative cartoons inspired by the lyrics of a famous hip-hop artist. With their big-breasted blondes and midget pimps, the drawings look like dirty cocktail napkins from a 1965 adult store.

"Our general theoretical concept," Mesler explains, "is that young people of our generation are really interested in high-end success—which is great, but they've left this wide-open field for the low-end, the middle ground."

"It's like, niche marketing," he adds.

Mesler moved Pruess Press to Bernard Street from a space on Chung King Road to a building shared with Daniel Hug and David

Kordansky galleries in October 2003. This expansion at Bernard Street occurred just before everything in Chinatown changed. They opened the gallery complex in 1999, just after Giovanni Intra and Steve Hanson founded China Art Objects. By 2001, the Chinatown "phenomenon" was already well known, with adulatory press about the New Bohemia appearing everywhere from *The Wall Street Journal* to *W* magazine. Recalling one of China's early shows—a videotape by Frances Stark of her cat listening to Black Flag in her apartment—the artist Laura Owens told a reporter, "It was incredibly compelling, but you didn't know whether it was art or not, and that was so exciting; it hadn't been defined yet."

Mesler and his friends don't have art school debt, and they're less invested in commercial art world success. They christened the space by summoning Art Bell, the high priest of conspiracy theorists and flying saucer believers, who for many years guided his insomniac fans through the night with *Coast to Coast AM*, his late-night radio show. Bell spelled out a message on Mesler's old Ouija board—*I'm here*—and that was enough. After wasting two years at the San Francisco Art Institute pursuing an art Career in "Jewish Expressionism," Mesler moved to Chinatown in 2000 and opened his first gallery. "I never wanted to represent artists," Mesler says. "I had so many friends who weren't showing, I just thought I could help facilitate some projects. Because it was so cheap, I could exist without selling anything. People came to Pruess who weren't in the LA art school orbit at all. We'd just hang out and play guitar."

In collaboration with his friend, the sci-fi genius Mark von Schlegell (who edits *The Rambler*, a foundational LA journal of poetics, critical thought, and anonymized art world gossip, inspired by the eighteenth-century writer Samuel Johnson's self-publication of the same name), Mesler's program has become more programmatic. "I started to realize," he says, "I didn't like the idea of artists going alone into their studios to make their work—it's just so sterile. We wanted the energy of the production house, where the studio could be the marketplace." And so Pruess Press, pruesspress.com, and 2/3/2 Studios, their film production subsidiary, were born.

"Our theory," Mesler says, "is—we came here to work, we didn't come to hang around." Citing one of his artists, Rabbi Milkblood, Mesler adds, "If you shoot yourself in the left foot, the right foot gets strong." I wonder what else Rabbi Milkblood says? "Don't fuck with our orgasm." "We object," von Schlegell adds, "to things being made for consumption, not for use." Pruess Press produces artist multiples and books; Pruess Studios records music produced by Mesler, von Schlegell, and their many friends. Recently, Pruess produced a series of collaborative monoprints by the artists Henry Taylor, Andrew Hahn, and Jason Meadows. (Meadows makes a cameo appearance in Brown's *Pastorale* kissing Katie Brennan, who is Taylor's gallerist at ACME's Chinatown offshoot gallery, Sister. Sometimes the Los Angeles art world seems very small.) Spontaneous and improvised, their music defines a new genre they call Reality Rock. "We discovered that everybody is a rock star when you treat them like one," von Schlegell says, because "music offers another level of anonymity. Last night, Jon Pylypchuk and his wife Annette were playing music with us. She is a Mennonite, and at one point she made him go and get a hymnal. She was reading things from this hymnal, tearing up while we just played music to accompany her."

The songs—including freestyle soul sung by Henry Taylor—are broadcast on the gallery's website, pruesspress.com.

Not surprisingly, fast and cheap are the guiding principles of Pruess's 2/3/2 Studios. The group has just finished their first feature film, *My Dinner with Merlin* (2008), directed by von Schlegell's partner, the artist Frances Scholz. Written in two weeks, shot on location in three, and edited in two more, the film features cameo appearances by Dan Graham, Joan Jonas, and the writers Danzy Senna, Fanny Howe, and Norman Klein in an epic inspired by the King Arthur legend.

In opposition to the art market's incessant process of branding, a handful of ambulatory, anonymous art "collectives" have appeared in the last several years. Still, I can't think of any who pursue their mission with as much wit and fluidity as Pruess Press. With their ironically garage-band aesthetic, Mesler and friends paradoxically bring a seriousness and professionalism that until now has been lacking among those who sought alternatives to the hegemony of LA's "studio system," the high-profile MFA.

Not wanting to miss out on the market for higher art education, Pruess Press has also founded a school. "We call it SCA," Mesler explains, "because we had all this leftover stationery, certificates, and awards that said Southern Cantonese Association, so we figured, we won't have to make new ones." "There's an excellent student-teacher ratio," von Schlegell adds. "We have two students, and we have a lot of teachers." Since the school's inception, SCA faculty has included Frances Stark, Dennis Hollingsworth, and the late Giovanni Intra. "We put Thomas Pynchon on the faculty list, thinking if we did, he might show up," von Schlegell says. "Yeah," adds Mesler. "Is he still alive?"

■

Marnie Weber says, "I like to think about things beyond what you can see." We're in her upstairs studio, sitting in front of her collage *Woodland Creatures*. This extraordinary piece, and its companion *The Treehouse*, is part of Weber's new image-suite, *Spirit Girls* (2005). In *Woodland Creatures*, a woman in a long white dress reclines with both arms raised on a funeral bier laden with flowers. She's both protected and haunted by companion animals, some of whom are half human: a flying owl, an aproned bear, a sheep in sexy high heels. The moonlit night is tinged violet, like deadly nightshade, that most delicious, somnambulant poison.

Weber is an artist who's known and highly respected among other artists. Collaborating with friends from Sonic Youth and Destroy All Monsters, Mike Kelley and Jim Shaw's LA art rock band, she's been around LA since the late 1980s, when she staged gallery performances and sang. Too original and singular to ever be lauded as LA art's "next big thing," she's nevertheless exhibited her prolific body of work continuously for about twenty years. Inspired by the freedom of the French surrealists, whose work she adores, Weber has devised a constantly evolving lexicon of images that references itself as more than art criticism, philosophy, or other art.

During the late 1990s she collaged pornographic images into pastoral landscapes. "[The models] carry the stigma of their past, but I'm trying to give them a new life—it's like saving a lost puppy," she told Darcey Steinke in *Spin*. Lately, though, she's decided to stop using found images. Pornography got old, particularly once she had a daughter. "Once I became a mother," Weber says, "I couldn't see the girls as figures anymore. I'd always seen them in a figurative, art historical sense—figures in a landscape. But once I had a little girl, I started seeing them as grown-up little girls. And that was the end. It stopped." Harking back to her performance days, she plays many of the characters herself. The rest of them, she casts and then costumes, poses, and directs. With a five-thousand-square-foot studio/soundstage in Glendale that she shares with her artist husband, Jim Shaw, two costume rooms, and a retinue of female assistants, Weber's production apparatus is reminiscent of silent movie studio days.

"I thought," she says of *Spirit Girls*, "it would be a nice idea to do a series about girls who've died and then come back to put on a musical. No, they aren't hungry ghosts! They've come back to spread a message. They're communicating, putting out. The spirit girls are all fictitious characters. I play the lead."

"But what about the animals in *Woodland*," I ask?

"I like the role of animals because they're always protecting. They're always gathering around. A girl is being guided into different situations. The animals create a male alter ego, without using an actual man. That's their primary function. They're idealized men."

I notice the chubby gremlin, his hips jutting out in the foreground, grasping a long pearl necklace made out of eggs. "Ah, he's the egg stealer. He steals eggs, which is kind of funny, but also tragic. All women come across the egg stealer at some point in their lives. The passing of time, loss of fertility, miscarriage, getting older—there are many ways."

Later, Weber walks me around the house. Her assistant, Tamara Sussman, is busy in the living room, cutting red roses out of colored contact sheets. Stuffed horses prance across the keyboard of an old piano, and Barbies of all eras, laid out on a wrought-iron coffee table, sunbathe on the deck. Downstairs in the basement, there's a witchy-looking metal soup bowl full of cut-out butterflies and women's faces. "Oh"—Weber laughs—"that's my next series there."

Driving down from Weber's house through Highland Park, a mural of enormous toucan parrots graces Birdman Pet Shop's concrete block wall. Behind the counter of El Pavo Bakery, there's a half-moon-shaped painting of a peacock whose enormous half-spread tail threatens to eclipse the mountain in the background. The sign reads MONTERREY. Outside again, I start to see the Figueroa Boulevard storefront windows, with their infant shoes and christening dress displays, in a new way.

■

Later that night, returning from my friend Matias Viegener's Silver Lake house, I see a guy step out the passenger-side door of a silver BMW on Sunset. A girl in a shiny silver rayon blouse is waiting for him on the sidewalk. He kisses her. The light turns green. The car ahead of me turns right onto Parkman, then right again, and disappears down the alley behind the Tropical. In certain frames of mind, each passing action or sight feels portentous. Sometimes I think the great difference between London or New York and LA is that less of it has been mythologized by poets and writers. Beyond the treacherous film-noir curves of Mulholland Drive and the gaping immaculate suburbs of daytime TV, how much do we know of LA? Vast tracts of the City remain unexplored. No mid-twentieth-century New York City cobblestone has been left unturned by the thousands of writers who lived there, but LA has yet to be thoroughly chronicled. Nothing is left to remind us of the populous boarding house world in downtown LA's Bunker Hill, bulldozed almost five decades ago to make way for the city's new high-rising skyline—nothing except for the stories of John Fante, and most of his work is out of print now.

Still, often, driving around LA, I'm struck by the slight artifacts of what I imagine as the city's utopian future. An otherwise generic office building in the mid-Wilshire district boasts three limestone friezes that celebrate labor, with human hands turning the earth, wielding a pickax, and pouring medicine into a beaker.

Low water washes between rocks and branches in an enormous, anonymous mural at the Wilshire Colonnade. Seals perch on rocky ledges; a flock of doves flies overhead. Two women and two men lounge among dry branches with their children. One man plays guitar. They're immigrants—Mexican and Scandinavian—the women have round breasts and shoulders; the men are slightly built: not the uber-proles of socialist realism, but quiet urban workers. It's another vision of heaven—dreamed of by trade union and social reformers who flocked here between the wars from harsh northeastern industrial cities—as compelling to them as Delia Brown's *Pastorale* seems to us now.

Public artworks like this summon a vision of a radiant city where working people dwelt in urbanity, leisure, and grace. Who put them here? "The myth of Los Angeles during the 1920s was that it could be a worker's paradise," says the writer and urban archaeologist Norman Klein. "It was the last city where you could work and buy a house. There was no labor movement here to speak of, but the promise LA made was that workers might enjoy an elegance and stability unknown in other cities."

During the 1930s Los Angeles pioneered one of the largest educational infrastructures in the country. The verdant, sprawling campuses of junior and community colleges, built when land was cheap, are reminders of a time when public education functioned as a new religion. Klein has made a study of LA's "history of forgetting." "The city," he says, is characterized by "moments of manic anxiety among its elite and policy makers. Like a house badly cleaned by a manic depressive, this city—its fantastic architecture, its lopsided infrastructure—is filled with half-completed episodes, lots of unwrapped junk that are clues to a larger emotional, collective confusion. LA is a neurotic's version of the planned city that keeps losing its way."

■

"It's flattering to kind of keep that hope alive," the painter Henry Taylor says. We're sitting in his Chinatown live/work studio on Hill Street, and he's talking about the monoprints he did last week at Pruess Press. "Joel is so encouraging, so positive. We're drawing late into the night. It makes you feel you're living a fuller life, the kind of life you've always wanted to be living."

Taylor, whose recent New York show at Daniel Reich in Chelsea sold out before the opening, has lived in Chinatown for fifteen months. Before that, he was "kind of floating" between Culver City, Santa Cruz, and Thousand Oaks, making paintings on the backs of cigarette packs when his studio was a kitchen table. Like all of his larger works, they're sharp and sweet, blatant, simple narrative images that conjure more complex histories.

While Taylor talks a mile a minute, my eyes are wandering through the forty to fifty finished works around his studio. Like the painter R. B. Kitaj, many of his paintings are compositionally disjunctive narratives, but Taylor packs a more aggressive visual punch. Painted in deep colors, his people practically burst through the frame. The first one that sucks me in is a painting of a young Black man in a T-shirt standing in front of a long, low Walmart building. Underneath the figure, a soldier crouches in a tunnel. It's any urban neighborhood, USA. "Yeah," says Taylor, "it's just kind of projects and stores. My brother was what they called a 'tunnel rat' in Vietnam—he was shot in the leg, and he was in a ditch. I used to read his letters to my mother because she couldn't read, and he'd write things like 'Mom, I'm really scared, I can't let the others know how scared I am.' And I was like, How could you be a damned soldier? I had two brothers who went to Nam. My other brother, Herschel, was shot there three times, he was shot on his birthday ... He said he was scared but dared not say it to the other younger soldiers he was in charge of. When I did my last show in New York, it was really like bringing my family with me. I was just thinking of him...."

While he was still a student at CalArts during the mid-'90s Taylor made a series of paintings inspired by the labels on bulk foods distributed to welfare clients: *US Dept. of Agriculture—Not to Be Sold or Exchanged.* He grew up in Oxnard, California, in a family of seven siblings, and one of his teachers at junior college, a CalArts grad, convinced Taylor that he should finish his BFA at that school. "I didn't know what they were talking about at art school," Taylor recalls of CalArts theory-centric reading lists. "I was like, did everybody read this shit?" Numerous other CalArts grads, such as Julie Becker and Andrea Bowers, who've gone on to become great artists, feel the same way. Taylor paints cars and hairstyles, Olde English beer cans, fat women, birds, and smiling Arabs. "I work intuitively," Taylor says, "just moving shit around."

We walk around the room to a painting of a thin man sitting in a Queen Anne chair. White shirt, black tie. There's a black horse behind him, and two guns on the table, like exhibits laid out for the court. "This is my grandfather," Taylor says. "He was a horse trainer, his name is Ardmore. He was shot and killed at thirty-three, ambushed in Naples in East Texas. My dad, whenever he got drunk, he would act out the scene: my dad was nine years old, and he went and picked up the body with my grandmother. His horse would not leave him. The horse was trying to protect him."

In between attending international art fairs, Taylor has recently begun a series of paintings of former Black Panther leaders. There's a blowup of the cover of George Jackson's book, *Soledad Brother.* A painting of Malcolm X, measuring the string for a cat's cradle while gazing straight ahead at the viewer. *Neighborhood Watch*, the painting says in black letters above Malcolm's head. As a child, Taylor had seen one of his brothers gravitate toward the Black Panther movement in Oakland. Taylor recalls: "I was too young to be a participant, but my brother was. He was involved in the struggle. Driving past Soledad Prison when I was in Santa Cruz got me thinking about Jackson. I reread the book and realized little has changed, if not gotten worse. I was just thinking about what people's priorities are now compared to those days. I'm still just curious, and I try to be sincere about learning."

■

Twenty-five blocks northeast of Chinatown at the Brewery Art Colony, LA's first artist-loft conversion, Eugenia P. Butler is reinventing the kind of process art she grew up with as the daughter of renowned Los Angeles gallerist Eugenia Butler Sr. Butler Sr. introduced the Fluxus art group to LA and represented such artists as Ed Kienholz, Joseph Kosuth, and John Baldessari. Butler remained in LA and became an artist herself. As she recalls, throughout the 1960s "there was this flow of electricity. Everything happened in the studio. We had the sensibility that we could change the world. That ideas were incredibly important." At that time, Butler and her friends—the artists James Lee Byars, Grant Cooper, and Eric Orr—were experimenting with light, body sounds, absence, and negative space. Staging impromptu happenings with ruby lasers on abandoned boulevards, inserting plaques bearing the description A CONGRUENT REALITY onto sidewalks, Butler's group opposed the static nature of minimalism. "I was interested," Butler says, "in how you could make work without that lugubrious materiality."

After having a child, Butler left LA and the art world for South America, where she studied shamanism. Returning in the late 1970s, she lived for a while in Beverly Hills and designed furniture. Now she lives at the Brewery and thinks mostly about the future, rarely the past.

In 1993 she began an ongoing work, *Fire in the Library*, in which she stages conversations between scientists, philosophers, writers, activists, psychiatrists, and filmmakers. In 2004 she launched *A Laboratory with Velocity: The First of a Series of Conversations on Envi-*

sioning the Future. The projects represent an extraordinary confluence between Fluxus-style art happenings, conventional think tanks, and academic panels. She pursues this work with real passion. To Butler, dialogue, although immaterial, is a living thing. "Dialogue," she tells me, "was such a formative element of how I learned about making art. I could see this really beautiful transmission of ideas between one human being and another, and I noticed the way these ideas would morph and change, become something else through that person's interior dialogue. I never felt territorial about any of this. I did not believe in it."

In *Laboratory with Velocity*, she hopes to get 250,000 people in LA thinking about the future. "When we think about the future in concrete terms," she says, "our reptile brains begin to work. It's a piece that's socially ambitious as well as artistically ambitious. Because I realized, now, that no one feels they have a right to think about the future, in some terrifying way. A dying body doesn't think about the future. But the Enrons and the Halliburtons are thinking about the future. What is our heart's desire? If we are going to hand on a future that's going to be livable to the next generation, we have to think about it now."

Butler thinks primarily as a visual artist. The walls of her large studio are strewn with drawings of concepts and thoughts. "Drawings," she says, "are how I move the work, the way I gather my ideas."

Walking around the room among Butler's many drawings, I see that they're written and painted on poster-board and large sheets of oak tag paper. They look like placards from a school science fair. Swirls of paint, newsprint cutouts, collaged photographs of animals organized within mismatched hierarchies into diagrams. She lists "five conditions":

1. seemingly ineradicable danger
2. ongoing threat
3. seeing our way to a healthier habitat
4. need to act
5. seeing the next step

One poster features the word *Mystery* in luxurious cursive script beside a lab beaker. "Intrigue," the work states, "story, romance, political, mystical, piecing together solutions." There are spirals and flowers and rainbow swirls, puce-green Magic Marker drawings. Moon craters—and above them she writes "fecund emptiness."

Since the first *Velocity* event, staged in November 2004, Butler has produced a short film, a DVD, twenty videotaped interviews, and a series of ten smaller dinners in which participants and those she calls "the Audience of Active Listeners" converse informally. It is an all-consuming process. Dozens of small events occur, then multiply, and then somehow inform each other. Sensitive to the intangible value of the fleeting daily exchanges that comprise the life of a city, Eugenia P. Butler has transformed civic discourse into conceptual artwork.

The people I visited on this short walk are only seven among thousands of artists now living in Los Angeles. Their lives make me believe that despite LA's famed "isolation," people here are creating not just the artifacts known as artworks but something much more elusive: a community of shared references, jokes, and indiscriminately wasted time that past centuries referred to as "culture." Yet each walk yields something new, and perhaps you'll take one of your own.

Jhumpa Lahiri

Jhumpa Lahiri is an expatriate American writer based in Italy. She launched her career with the short story collection *Interpreter of Maladies*, which introduced several of the recurring themes that she maintained in her 2008 collection *Unaccustomed Earth*, and her novels *The Namesake* (2003) and *The Lowlands* (2013): the movement of migrants between different cultural worlds, the overlap of personal and family histories with immediate anxieties and social problems, and the vexed question of assimilation. Lahiri also returns to several of these themes in her frequent essays for magazines like the *New Yorker*—and it is hard not to notice the overlap between Lahiri's fiction and nonfiction, both in terms of shared content and style (many of her essays could be mistaken for short stories). Where Lahiri's earlier fiction drew on her family's experience (Berngali parents moving to London; the whole family moving to the US when Lahiri was three), her more recent career has been defined by a different relocation—Lahiri's move to Rome in 2011, which saw the author switch to writing in Italian, so that her book of essays *In Other Words* (2016) was published in facing Italian and English, while her latest novel, *Whereabouts* (2021), was originally published in Italian as *Dove mi trovo* (2018). Her reflections on Simon Dinnerstein's painting reflect her insistent inquiry into the relationship between place, belonging, personal history, and form, with some particularly detailed reflections on the triptych's complex use of narrative and time.

The Space between the Pictures

I first met Simon Dinnerstein in a letter of introduction delivered to me by a mutual friend I'd invited to tea. In the letter, Simon wrote kindly about my writing and, venturing to suggest that I might find his painting *The Fulbright Triptych* "of interest," invited me to contribute an essay for this book [*The Suspension of Time*]. Along with the letter he sent a catalog of his work and a reproduction of the triptych, measuring fourteen-and-a-half by eleven inches. I spent that summer evening looking at the pages of the catalog. There were paintings and drawings of women sleeping and dreaming. Facades of Victorian row houses in Brooklyn, where Simon and I both live, on streets that I'd walked along. I saw a little girl sitting at a piano. A flower market in Rome. One painting, of a nude mother and child lying head to toe in bed against a vivid persimmon wall, reminded me of the portraits of Balthus. A few days later I wrote back to Simon by e-mail, accepting his invitation, and taped the reproduction of *The Fulbright Triptych* to a wall in the room where I write.

The painting depicts an artist's studio, a place where creative work is produced. It is, specifically, a printmaker's workshop. The central panel, about twice the width of the two on either side, contains a black table positioned in front of two radiators set into alcoves in the wall. The table is arrayed with engraving tools, objects vaguely reminiscent of a surgeon's instruments. A copperplate, resembling the solid halos of Giotto's angels, rests ever so slightly off center, on top of a square leather pad. Above the table, a pair of windows reveals a single landscape of homes and hills and sky, the vista divided in equally sized sections by the windows' frames. In the left panel, a barefoot woman with short, dark hair sits with a naked baby girl in her lap. In the right panel, a man sits alone. The man and woman look directly at the viewer. The child's gaze, lighter than those of her parents, strays to one side. Two houseplants, similar but not identical, hang from nails at the same height above the man's and woman's heads. The man's clothing—striped blue-and-white pants, laced work

Simon Dinnerstein,
The Fulbright Triptych,
1971–74, oil on wood panels, 14 feet in width, framed and separated, Palmer Museum of Art, Pennsylvania State University, gift of the Friends of the Palmer Museum of Art.
© Simon Dinnerstein. Courtesy of the artist.

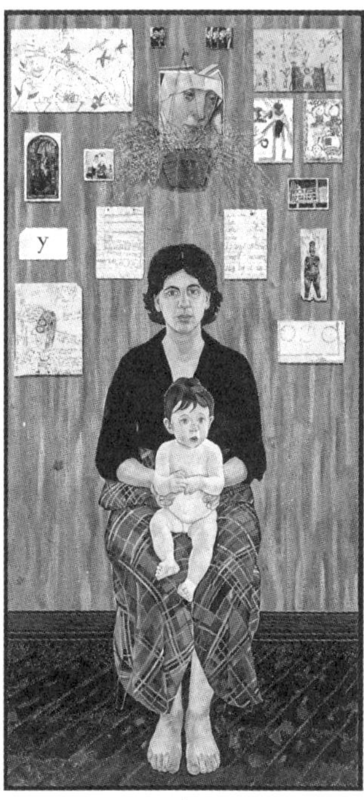

boots, a wide brown belt, a navy shirt with a wide collar—evoke the early 1970s, when I myself was a child. The painting is both a self-portrait and a family portrait; the man is Simon, the woman is his wife, Renée, and the baby is their daughter, Simone.

There are only three things the three panels have in common. The first is the floor made of thickly scabbed wooden planks. The second is the wallpaper, which has muddy peach and tan and green stripes seemingly applied with a paintbrush, and is patterned with tiny dots that lend it a perforated quality. The third is an assembly of small images, mostly visual but some consisting of text, decorating these papered walls. There are postcards of paintings, many of which I recognize: Bellini, Ingres, Hans Holbein, Degas. There are family photographs, some playfully taken in a photo booth, along with quotations, letters, things written on sheets of ruled paper, children's drawings. Each of these items, fifty-six in total, appears to be literally pasted to the surface in the manner of a collage, but is, in fact, a painted replica.

I have collected postcards of paintings since I was a teenager. And from the time I first set up a desk and started writing in my early

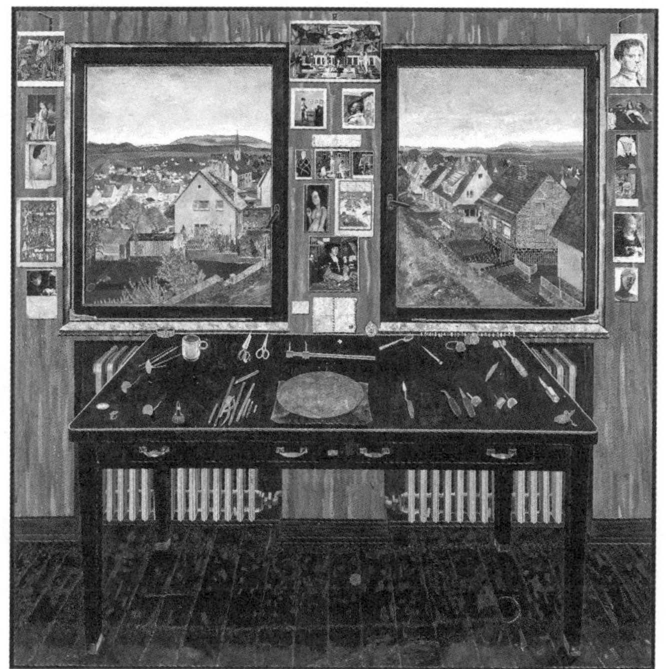
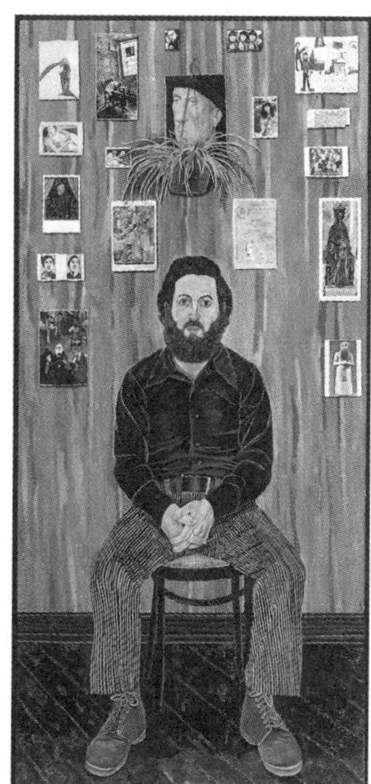

twenties, I have marked my creative territory with a version of the informal, idiosyncratic two-dimensional gallery displayed on the walls of *The Fulbright Triptych*. These are the things that comfort my eyes when they wander from page or screen, that witness my solitary labor day after day. Currently, against the backdrop of teal-blue walls, there is a large map of Massachusetts, the place where I set many of my stories, and a smaller map, recently xeroxed from the New York Public Library, of the neighborhood in Calcutta where my father was raised, a place I am currently struggling to conjure. There are drawings, copied by my own hand from photographs of my parents and husband and children, quotations from Nathaniel Hawthorne and from Corinthians 13. There are postcards of work by Piero della Francesca, Giorgio Morandi, and Phillip Guston. Pictures of Virginia Woolf, Anne Sexton, and Hilda Doolittle. A blue-and-orange Joan Mitchell painting I ripped out of a magazine, called *Merci*, the brilliant hues faded from exposure to direct sunlight. A letter, propped up so that I can see it behind the screen of my laptop, sent to me from Paris by Mavis Gallant. As my desks and sources of inspiration have changed over the years, so have the things with which I've chosen to surround myself. But when they are on the walls of the place where I write, they become talismanic; to be forced to take them down and box them up in the course of a move always feels like a sort of death.

■

About two months after receiving Simon's letter, I went with my friend Tonuca—the friend who had brought me his letter—to visit him in Park Slope. Located a short distance from the neighborhood I live in now, Park Slope is deeply familiar to me. For five years I lived less than three blocks away from Simon's home, in an apartment where I brought my son, and then my daughter, home from the hospital after they were born. For those years, I probably bought my milk, bagels, and cups of coffee from the same shops along Seventh Avenue, Park Slope's commercial thoroughfare, as Simon.

The man who welcomed us was nearly forty years older than the one sitting in the *Triptych*. His hair and beard were gray, and he wore glasses, black jeans, and a black button-down shirt. Renée was at home that day as well, her hair still short, though no longer the ebony shade Simon had painted it. We stood on the spacious parlor floor which has a large, beautiful kitchen at one end and a gleaming grand piano at the other (Simon and Renée's daughter, the little girl he had drawn at the piano, grew up to be a concert pianist who used to give lessons to Tonuca's daughter).

As we looked at the many paintings and drawings in the room, I was overwhelmed by the personal history of people I barely knew, by the passage of time cycling forward and back. For there was a drawing of Simone, the unclothed infant in the *Triptych*, as a grown woman, eight months pregnant with her son, her shirt unbuttoned to reveal the skin of her swollen belly, her face and body filled with a weary satisfaction. The young couple in the *Triptych*, just setting out on the journey of parenthood, were grandparents now. And just as that brand-new family who had been keeping me company on the wall of my writing room has since spawned another, so the artist in the early years of his creative life now lives in a house chockablock with the work he has produced, hanging up and leaning against just about every wall.

Simon was generous with his time, serious but unassuming. He spoke candidly about his art, his life, his interests, his dreams. He talked about the years he and his family had spent in Rome at the American Academy. His love of reading was frequently conveyed. He recommended *Blindness* by José Saramago, and showed me a painting that he feels has a connection with Bulgakov's *The Master and Margarita*. He spoke of Strindberg's *A Dream Play* and of *Tonio Kröger*, a novella by Thomas Mann. I'd read the story over twenty years ago, in college, and remembered it dimly. Simon spoke of it with such enthusiasm that I reread it as soon as I got home.

The visit concluded in Simon's studio. Like mine, it is located on the top floor of a row house. Compared to the other rooms I'd seen, the studio was grittier, untouched by renovation, the plaster walls cracked. Lights were clamped to poles, overlapping blue-and-green tape was stuck to the floorboard, and fluorescent panels hung from the flaking ceiling. On dirtied white walls were hooks from which nothing hung. Midday sun shone into three south-facing windows, one of the panes broken. Through them the colors of autumn were visible, just beginning to grace the leaves of the trees. We could hear the voices of children calling out as they played on the grounds of P.S. 321, the school where Renée taught for many years.

Simon showed us his recent work, a series painted literally onto his palettes, along with something much older—two charcoal drawings he had made of Renée, nude, when she was pregnant with Simone, an uncanny reverse echo of the drawing of Simone, similarly pregnant and bearing distinct resemblance to her mother, downstairs. One of the newer paintings, like the *Triptych*, featured a window. Only instead of revealing the world outside, a self-portrait filled much of the frame, and looked in at the viewer.

I am loath to admit people into the room where I work and was struck by Simon's willingness to allow us to gather there and chat. I saw his curled-up tubes of paint, his easels. Brushes arrayed like beheaded flower stems in an Italian coffee can. Chairs where his models have sat. And tucked into an alcove, taped to one wall, a living continuum of the backdrop of the *Triptych*: a collection of reproduced works of art in the form of postcards and newspaper clippings, many of them faded from sun and age.

■

In December 2008, two months after meeting Simon in person, I accompanied him to Penn State University, where *The Fulbright Triptych* resides in the Palmer Museum of Art. Along for the ride were Virginia Bonito, an art historian, and a curator at the National Academy, Marshall Price. In the course of the four-hour drive, much of which crosses through the milky, monotonous landscape of northeastern and central Pennsylvania, I asked Simon to talk about the genesis of the painting. He said that he had begun it in 1971, in Germany, when he was twenty-eight years old. He had traveled to Germany the year before, with Renée, thanks to a Fulbright fellowship. He had proposed to study the work of Dürer. After working on the middle panel for six months, drawing forms in black Rapidograph on gessoed wood, he returned to Brooklyn where, after two-and-a-half-years, the painting was finished in 1974. He recalled that the apartment in Germany where the painting was conceived came unfurnished. The black table in the central panel was given to him by his landlord and became his subject. It was his first painting. Until then, he had made drawings.

Simon told us that the *Triptych* changed his life before it was even finished. When it was still in progress, when he was struggling to pay a rent of ninety dollars a month and support his wife and child, he walked unbidden into New York's Staempfli Gallery and managed to get the dealer and his co-director, Phillip Bruno, to visit his studio in Brooklyn. After looking at the painting for twenty minutes and not saying a word, the dealer, George Staempfli, told Simon that he wanted to own it. He then proposed an arrangement: he would pay Simon a fixed sum every month until it was finished, and then he would exhibit it. It was an extraordinary stroke of good fortune, a moment that forever altered Simon's life and career. As he recounted the story, it was clear that the memory still overwhelmed him.

I understood his emotion well. Any artist lucky enough to migrate from obscurity to recognition, from poverty to solvency, knows what a miracle it is. Recognition, combined with the ability to support oneself as much as possible on one's creative work, is what aspiring artists dream of. But once achieved, the new reality itself feels like a dream. This is how I have felt for the past dozen years, after a door, against similar odds, opened for me, enabling me to make my living as a writer. Listening to Simon, I realized I would feel this way for the rest of my life. I asked Simon what he'd been reading when he started the painting. The answer was *Moby-Dick*. He'd read Melville's novel for the entire year he was in Germany, repeatedly renewing it from the library. Still not finished when he was scheduled to sail back to America, he brought the book back with him and finished it, poetically, on the high seas before mailing it back to the library in Europe. He told me another thing: that on the back of the central panel of the *Triptych*, Renée had nailed a five-mark coin to the wood crossbars, corresponding to the gold coin Ahab nails to the mast of the *Pequod*. "Begun in Good Faith and High Hopes on May 3rd, 1971 . . . with the love of Renée" is written in her hand beneath the coin. The benediction touched me; I remembered my own shaky beginnings as a writer, and how much my husband's faith in me meant at the time.

It is striking, and also fitting, that a novel so distinctly American, a novel about appearance and reality, about Ishmael's reflective wandering and Ahab's quest, informs the creation of the *Triptych*. For this is a painting, among other things, about what it means to be an artist: a necessary combination of Ishmael's absorption of the world, fused with Ahab's passion. It is also an intensely personal painting, just as *Moby-Dick*, for all its vastness, is an intensely personal narrative. It is a painting about a young American artist's absorption of northern Europe art, about his study of Dürer's copper engravings, about his response to that discipline in a new medium, and about his journey home. The triptych-in-progress not only crossed the Atlantic physically along with its creator, but embodies dense layers of crossings between past and present, between the real and the re-created. Between emerging and being, and between conception and birth.

It had been almost nine years since Simon had seen the *Triptych*. It is not the same for writers, who are able to revisit their work simply by pulling it off a shelf. As we sat in a restaurant in University Park, about to head over to the Palmer, I felt a vicarious sense of nervous anticipation. It was as if we were going to visit a child who had both grown unrecognizably old and stayed exactly the same. The people at the museum were expecting us, and the panels had been brought into a special room for us to view, the fourteen inches I'd gotten to know in reproduction now stretched to fourteen feet. The first thing Simon said when he saw it was that the panels needed to be set further apart.

Once they were arranged to his satisfaction, we stood far and close, taking notes and photographs. For me the pleasure of seeing a real painting has to do with those textures and details that lie dormant in reproduction. Face-to-face, I became aware of the roughness of the subfloor, the seams of the wallpaper. The veins on Renée's feet, the sheen of her plaid skirt. The bold swirls in Simon's hair, the rich velvet of his shirt, the fiery flecks in his beard. With the lights adjusted a particular way, I saw how brightly the copperplate, painted in gold leaf, shone. Most significant was the detail of the windowsills, splattered with paint, turning the windows into easels, and thus turning the view they contained into a paradox: something both beyond and within the room, something that is both reality, passively seen, and art, actively re-created.

Another aspect of the painting I was appreciating for the first time was the extent to which the painting represents a compression of real space and time. The room we see, albeit broken into three sections, is neither an apartment in Germany nor a studio in Brooklyn, but an amalgamated realm that is another place altogether. The view through the windows is of the German countryside, but the floor and the wallpaper, the hanging plants, the sycamore fronds scattered on the worktable, are native to Brooklyn. Now that I knew the full story—that Renée was not yet pregnant when Simon started working on the *Triptych*, but that by the time he finished it, Simone had been born—the painting's narrative became apparent. In this sense it is as much a trilogy as it is a triptych, for the painting shows us a life in stages, in parts. It shows what exists, and what does not, and what existed only previously. It reminded me of instances in my writing when, working from the past, I have had to manipulate actual events in order to serve the purpose of fiction. *The Fulbright Triptych* is the first time I appreciated this deliberate rearrangement of reality on a visual level.

Simon talked about many of the items, depicted in astonishing precision, on the walls of the painting. He read a poem written by a thirteen-year-old girl named Gloria Mintz:

Grey and sweating / And only one I person / Fighting and fretting.

He pointed out a ballpoint drawing by one of Renée's students, and reading exercises they had done. He read a quotation about language, and asked us to guess who it was attributed to (I guessed Plato; the answer was Wittgenstein). There was a letter propped up between the windows, and Simon crouched down, offering to read it, stepping into the world of the painting as if it were a stage set (it is three-quarters life-size). It was a letter to Simon from Renée, who at one point during their years in Germany had gone back to New York to visit her ailing father. She recounted an anxiety dream about being pregnant, a dream she'd had before the painting was conceived.

The things on the wall would be different now, Simon told us, but I saw that his love for them had not waned. Nor had their presence; they were there, an artist's ephemera made permanent, painted into the wood. They were all sacred to him, everything from the work of van Eyck and Seurat to a colorful drawing by two German girls, daughters of a couple the Dinnersteins had befriended in the town, named Simone and Andrea. Simon told us that Simone Dinnerstein (whose name is pronounced Simona) was named after these two girls, and that after she was born, six-year-old Andrea sent them the drawing as a baby gift. As I stood in front of the panel on the right, he pointed, standing directly in front of his painted younger self, to a re-created paragraph torn from the re-created ivory page of a re-created book. "Do you recognize this?" he asked. I shook my head at first, then stopped when I read, "To me, the white whale is that wall, shoved near to me. Sometimes I think there's naught beyond." It was a passage from chapter 36 of *Moby-Dick*.

■

A painting of an artist's studio is an inherent contradiction, and a profoundly intimate thing. It is a finished work that represents something impossible to represent—the piecemeal, protracted process of making art. To work as an artist is to revisit something day after day, to look at a subject or an experience not twice or twenty times but what easily feels like twenty thousand times. In the course of those repeated visits, the thing seen—or in a writer's case, contemplated—begins necessarily to evolve, to become something other than itself, to become, at times, unrecognizable. The walls of the studio, the floor, the furniture, the scraps taped to the walls are what remain constant, and they are as revealing, as much of a self-portrait, as the depiction of an artist's figure or face. In that sense, *The Fulbright Triptych* is a self-portrait twice over.

One of the postcards on the walls of the *Triptych*, of a painting by Vermeer, is a self-portrait of the artist seated at his easel, his back to the viewer, working with a model who poses in the background. But the artist in *The Fulbright Triptych* sits still, a figure who is both model and artist, his fingers interlaced, the instruments on his worktable untouched. That he is not actively occupied is, of course, an illusion. The completed painting, the enduring distillation of the effort required to create that composed figure, reminds us of this. After getting to know Simon a little bit, I think that his posture in the painting, at once vigilant and relaxed, is appropriate. He is a man who not only paints the world he sees but deeply thinks about and questions it—thoughts and questions that eventually become manifest in his work. His presence in the painting reminds us that the idle moments in one's studio, when one is not actively painting or writing or making anything, when one is perhaps sitting in a chair staring into space, are precisely the moments inspiration tends to strike.

I love *The Fulbright Triptych* and will continue to keep a reproduction of it taped up in my writing room, because it is about the interplay of the two aspects of my life that are the most sacred to me: art and family. When I was first getting to know the painting, I regarded it as a fugue of threes. The three panels, the three figures. The three formal subjects, portraits, still life, landscape. The three levels of representation—the painting, the reproductions of other paintings, the painted renditions of those reproductions. After looking at the painting and thinking about it for nearly six months, I see that it is as much about dyad as triads, and about the primal alchemy of two becoming three. The painting is about a marriage and about the consequence of that marriage: a child. It is also about an individual who, doubly creative as artist and father, exists both in the realm of art and of life; who is devoted to both things but is also sundered by them, occupying a panel of his own. As a writer who is also the mother of two young children, I experience this sense of division on a daily basis. Though the artist's family exists within the *Triptych*, has even participated in its creation by posing for it, the painting is made by him alone, in the studio, outside ordinary life. In *Tonio Kröger* Mann writes: "The artist must be unhuman, extra-human; he must stand in a queer aloof relationship to our humanity; only so is he in a position, I ought to say only so would he be tempted, to represent it, to present it, to portray it to good effect."

As we were getting ready to leave the museum, there was a moment when Simon and I stood alone with his painting. "I believe the meaning of the painting is contained in the space between the pictures," Simon told me. Whether he was referring to the space between the reproductions he'd painted or the space between the panels themselves was not clear to me at the time. But in the process of writing this essay, I began to understand.

Ben Lerner

Ben Lerner is a Fulbright-award-winning poet (not to be confused with the Fulbright-award-winning poet, Adam Gordon, from Lerner's acclaimed first novel, *Leaving the Atocha Station* [2011]), and the author of three highly praised novels (though not to be confused with the highly praised novelist who narrates Lerner's second novel, *10:04* [2014]). Lerner's place at the vanguard of the contemporary resurgence in autofiction helps explain why so many of his essays are much more confessional than most of his peers'; along with his "jealousy" towards visual artists, Lerner has written a whole book on his *Hatred of Poetry* (2016), and, just like the narrator in the opening chapter of *Leaving the Atocha Station*, Lerner frequently reflects on his own inability to have "a profound experience of art." His essay on vandalism charts similar territory, with Lerner admitting that, "I've often felt threatened by vandals. I have secretly envied their passion and commitment, perhaps particularly the 'pathological' ones." The violence of vandals, as Lerner keenly catalogues—stabbing paintings with barriers that are intended to protect the artworks, writing or spray-painting them, shooting a series of prints, hitting things with a hammer, urinating on them—is often ostensibly motivated by a desire to improve them (either conceptually, or in terms of financial value), but it is the intense, often physical response that artworks provoke in vandals that most fascinates him here. As in Lerner's novels, when it comes to vandalism, the line between love and destruction is very thin indeed.

Damage Control

Much of the story of twentieth-century art can be told as a series of acts of vandalism. Cubist collage attacked the expectation that a painting should look like something in the world. "In my case," Picasso said, "a picture is a sum of destructions." Abstract painters criticized Cubism for not going far enough: "Cézanne broke the fruit dish," Robert Delaunay reportedly said, "and we should not glue it together again, as the Cubists do." Marcel Duchamp, not satisfied with assaulting painting from within, abandoned the medium after 1918, turning his attention to the presentation of ready-made objects as art, the most infamous of which was the urinal, entitled *Fountain*, he submitted to the American Society of Independent Artists under the pseudonym "R. Mutt" for its inaugural exhibition, in 1917. Whatever else Duchamp's gesture was—a provocative way of blurring the boundary between art and mundane objects, a critique of the idea of authorship—it was also a metaphoric micturition on the history of creative expression. Another work of Duchamp's, *L.H.O.O.Q.*, consisted of a cheap postcard-size reproduction of the *Mona Lisa*, on which he drew a mustache and goatee. Pronounced aloud in French, the title sounds like *Elle a chaud au cul*, which translates colloquially to something along the lines of "She's horny." Duchamp's focus was on degradation, setting the stage for the deskilled and frequently scatological experiments of a range of progeny, from Dubuffet to Warhol to the Andres Serrano *Piss Christ* that so pissed off Jesse Helms.

As a kid, when I first saw images of Jackson Pollock at work, I thought I was watching somebody vandalize a painting, not create one: the canvas was on the floor, paint was splattered and poured, and he was indifferent to the ash falling from his cigarette. Trash—nails, tacks, buttons—can be found encrusted in his paintings' surfaces. In 1953, Rauschenberg erased a de Kooning drawing; now in the San Francisco MOMA, it's widely considered a landmark of postwar art—ghostly traces in a gilded frame. In 1966, Gustav Metzger and others hosted the Destruction in Art Symposium in London, inviting a number of participants, especially those who worked by burning, cutting, tearing, and blowing up. Metzger, the author of the manifesto "Auto-Destructive Art," conceived of such art as "an attack ... on art dealers and collectors who manipulate modern art for profit." Some in the London press referred to it simply as "organized vandalism." (Metzger's subversions were the subject of a 2011 retrospective at the New Museum, in New York.) One notable antecedent of the conference was the work of Jean Tinguely, whose giant "*méta-mécanique*" *Homage to New York* beat itself to death in the MoMA sculpture garden on March 17, 1960. Autodestruction was also a theme and technique in Body Art, performances in which flesh was medium: Yoko Ono inviting an audience to cut away her clothing; Vito Acconci biting himself; Chris Burden being shot, or nailed to a car.

Examples could be multiplied easily, almost endlessly—this highly selective catalogue only takes us up to the Seventies; what's clear is that modern art is inseparable from the destruction of modern art. Demolition, defacement, and debasement are not just fates artworks suffer at the hands of vandals; they're often what those works are. It's against this backdrop that vandals often claim to be artists—claim that they are moving the history of art forward by renovating received ideas or performing what artists and critics have come to call "institutional critique"—and that artists claim to be vandals, attacking the notion that art is property and ridiculing existing canons of taste. It's precisely when vandals and artists are so difficult to tell apart that an act of vandalism can raise important and often uncomfortable questions about how we really define and value art.

■

On Sunday, October 7, 2012, a twenty-six-year-old Polish man named Vladimir Umanets walked into the Tate Modern and wrote VLADIMIR UMANETS '12 A POTENTIAL PIECE OF YELLOWISM in the bottom right corner of Rothko's 1958 *Black on Maroon* with a black paint pen. It was an act made to be googled, and googling it led to Umanets's blog, which featured the so-called Yellowism manifesto, a work of Neo-Dadaist nonsense. Yellowism, the movement Umanets founded with his friend Marcin Łodyga, "is not art or anti-art":

> Examples of Yellowism can look like works of art but are not works of art. We believe that the context for works of art is already art. . . . Every piece of Yellowism is only about yellow and nothing more, therefore all pieces of Yellowism are identical in content—all manifestations of Yellowism have the same sense and meaning and express exactly the same. . . . Yellowism can be presented only in yellowistic chambers.

Umanets, who argued that he was working in the tradition of Duchamp, was resolute that his action was not vandalism, as he believed it increased the aesthetic and financial value of the Rothko:

> With my signature this work will be much more valuable a work of art and also financially, because I changed the meaning. Someone who removes this signature will be an asshole.

The previous June, Uriel Landeros, a twenty-two-year-old artist from Houston, approached Picasso's *Woman in a Red Armchair* in the city's Menil Collection and spray-painted a stenciled image of a matador and bull along with the word conquista onto the canvas. Landeros described his act as one of social and political defiance: "It's just a piece of cloth," he said. "What matters most is the people who are suffering." Another museumgoer filmed the attack on his cell phone; a guard appears just in time to insist that picture-taking is forbidden. Landeros's paintings were later exhibited at a gallery in Houston, an event that received more outraged attention than his tagging the Picasso. The decision to treat the vandal as a "legitimate" artist was almost universally condemned.

Umanets's and Landeros's acts recall other destructive performances in museums. In 1993, at the Carré d'Art in Nîmes, an exhibition included a copy of Duchamp's *Fountain*. On August 24, a sixty-three-year-old man named Pierre Pinoncelli urinated into the urinal, then hit it once with a small hammer before guards intervened. During the ensuing trial he explained that his "urinal happening" was intended to restore life to what had become a mere monument; as the critic Leland de la Durantaye explains, "When the prosecution accused him of 'vandalism,' he was indignant, claiming that, on the contrary, he had *added* value to the work." While the other urinals in circulation were "faceless replicas," this particular copy "now had a history and was thus immeasurably more valuable than before." (Urinating on a Duchamp is a mini-tradition: Yuan Cai and Jian Jun Xi, two British-Chinese artists, pissed on *Fountain* in 2000 at the Tate. "As Duchamp said himself, it's the artist's choice. He chooses what is art. We just added to it," Cai explained. Spray-painting a Picasso is also familiar: in 1974, Tony Shafrazi—then an artist, now a well-known art dealer—sprayed KILL LIES ALL on *Guernica*. "I wanted to bring the art absolutely up to date, to retrieve it from art history and give it life," he said at the time.)

Pinoncelli had already had a busy career. Among other undertakings, he'd doused the French culture minister André Malraux with red paint; he'd robbed a bank at gunpoint but taken only ten francs; he'd cut off the tip of one of his fingers in a performance in Colombia in protest against the FARC. On January 4, 2006, Pinoncelli again vandalized a Duchamp. This time the happening was sans urine: he walked into the Centre Pompidou and hit another replica with a hammer, then more or less repeated his original arguments at trial. The courts required him to pay more than €200,000 in damages.

Few, if any, were willing to take Pinoncelli's acts seriously as art. According to the art historian Dario Gamboni—the author of an excellent (and, interestingly, the only) book on modern art vandalism—when the French artist Benjamin Vautier (known simply as Ben) demanded that *Art Press* acknowledge the Nîmes attack as an artistic intervention, the editors replied:

> [He] has done all that only for the Press and not for art, he would have done anything to be talked about, one cannot inscribe his name in the history of art while removing every meaning except that of whimpering for publicity. (The translation from the French is Gamboni's.)

Gamboni himself questions Pinoncelli's claim to be an artist. "Pinoncelli," he says, "could not give a convincing internal explanation of his resorting not only to 'urine' but to a hammer" and "showed a poor knowledge" of the history of *Fountain*. While conceding that Pinoncelli is not necessarily "deranged," and that "the search for public acknowledgment" often motivates artists, Gamboni writes that "the importance of the attention-seeking element" in Pinoncelli's act, "as well as its lack of coherence and relevance from an 'artistic' point of view, bring it exceptionally close to the 'pathological' cases " of vandalism—cases like that of Laszlo Toth, who, believing himself to be the risen Christ, took a hammer to Michelangelo's *Pietà* in 1972.

How would showing that Pinoncelli's gesture of what he termed "creative destruction" was inconsistent, incoherent, unsophisticated, or even a little deranged prove that it was merely vandalism and not art? If a critic were to review a show in a gallery and find it incoherent and attention-seeking, she might contend that the work was horrible—but she would almost certainly assume that it was horrible art. Charges of incoherence and irrelevance are often leveled at artists without that making them vandals. It is quite easy to argue that Umanets and Landeros and Pinoncelli are *bad* artists—derivative, sloppy, stupid. And it is easy to argue that they are merely destructive—but then performative destruction has a long and sanctioned history in the avant-garde. (And not just the destruction of one's own work or an attack on an abstract idea. Recently, the British artists Jake and Dinos Chapman purchased, and then drew on, Goya prints, and this year Gaylen Gerber bought and painted over two ceramics by Lucio Fontana.) If we resort to claiming that what sets vandals apart is that they compromise valuable objects, that the originals aren't their property, or that they violate the contract between the museum and the public, we run up against the fact that the rejection of beauty and resistance to the market have been rhetorical staples of avant-garde art for half a century or more.

The speed with which artists and critics and institutions categorize figures like Pinoncelli as vandals and not radical artists betrays an open secret in the world of contemporary art: nobody is supposed to take those vanguard ideas *too* seriously. Like some kind of village idiot, a vandal takes literally what we're only supposed to pretend to believe: anything can be art, traditional media must give way to conceptual performance, and the money-hungry art world must be subject to ruthless critique.

■

I should admit that I've often felt threatened by vandals. I have secretly envied their passion and commitment, perhaps particularly the "pathological" ones. For many of my generation who grew up under the dominance of Warhol's cool, stylized stupidity, who grew up in an era Fredric Jameson said was characterized by the "waning of affect," the intensity of the vandal's response to an artwork can inspire a kind of anxiety, almost jealousy. Some vandals seem to suffer from something I've felt a little bad about not suffering from: Stendhal's syndrome.

According to the Italian psychiatrist Graziella Magherini, Stendhal's syndrome—also known as "hyperkulturemia" or "Florence syndrome"—is a psychosomatic condition in which museumgoers are overwhelmed by the presence of great art, resulting in a range of responses: breathlessness, panic, fainting, paranoia, disorientation. The condition is so named because of Stendhal's account of his visit to the Basilica of Santa Croce:

> I was already in a kind of ecstasy from the idea of being in Florence and the proximity of the great men whose tombs I had just seen. Absorbed in the contemplation of sublime beauty, I saw it close-up—I touched it, so to speak. I had reached that point of emotion where the heavenly sensations of the fine arts meet passionate feeling. As I emerged from Santa Croce, I had palpitations (what they call an attack of the nerves in Berlin); the life went out of me, and I walked in fear of falling.

When I visited Florence last summer, the life went out of me only because of the tourists; I couldn't see the art in the Uffizi for all the cameras. While Magherini does not link Stendhal's syndrome to acts of vandalism, others have speculated that some attacks on artworks might result from such bouts of supersensitivity.

The question that serves as the title for Barnett Newman's series of large canvases *Who's Afraid of Red, Yellow and Blue* was answered in a shockingly direct way by Josef Nikolaus Kleer on April 13, 1982. As Gamboni describes it, Kleer, a twenty-nine-year-old veterinary-medicine student, entered Berlin's Nationalgalerie through a rear entrance while the museum was closed, made his way to the room where a Newman canvas was hung, picked up one of the plastic rails that were arranged on the ground to keep visitors from getting too close to the painting, and struck the canvas violently. He also punched it and kicked it and spat on it. According to Gamboni:

> He then placed several documents on and around the damaged work: on its blue part, a slip of paper inscribed "Whoever does not yet understand it must pay for it! A small contribution to cleanness. Author: Josef Nikolaus Kleer. Price: on arrangement" and "Action artist"; on the ground in front of it, a copy of the last issue of the magazine *Der Spiegel*, with a caricature of the then British Prime Minister Margaret Thatcher ... ; in front of the red part, a copy of the "Red List," an official catalogue of remedies published by the German pharmaceutical industry; in front of the yellow part, a yellow housekeeping book with a second slip of paper carrying the inscription "Title: Housekeeping book. A work of art of the commune of Tietzenweg, attic on the right. Not to be sold"; finally, lying somewhere on the ground, a red cheque-book. These items enabled the police to find the culprit quickly.

Kleer's violence was motivated, he would maintain, not only by outrage that a work of art could cost so much but also by the intensely negative effect the canvas had on him. One significant inconsistency in Kleer's account of his attack is that he said it was inspired at once by a sense of Newman's fraudulence—Kleer believed himself "capable of making a comparable picture for a fraction of the acquisition price"—and by a sense of Newman's tremendous power: standing before the work, Kleer reported having felt an overwhelming fear.

Newman was interested in the sublime, not the beautiful—and sublimity has always been associated with terror, with the sensation of being undone, a "fear of falling." Kleer's use of part of the plastic barrier as a weapon is almost an ironic homage to Newman, who for a show at the Betty Parsons Gallery in 1951 posted a note on the wall that read: "There is a tendency to look at large pictures from a distance. The large pictures in this exhibition are intended to be seen from a short distance." Kleer refused all distance—"I touched it, so to speak." (Newman's canvases have been attacked several times since. Four years after Kleer battered *Who's Afraid of Red, Yellow and*

Blue IV, a thirty-one-year-old man named Gerard Jan van Bladeren slashed *Who's Afraid of Red, Yellow and Blue III* in Amsterdam's Stedelijk Museum with a knife. Eleven years later, at the same museum, he slashed Newman's *Cathedra*.)

Was Kleer so struck by the work that he had to strike back, just as, in 2007, a thirty-year-old woman, Rindy Sam, claimed to be so transported by a white panel of Cy Twombly's triptych *Phaedrus* that she spontaneously kissed it, smearing it with red lipstick? ("There is also a madness," Socrates says in his dialogue with Phaedrus, "which is a divine gift.") This hyperkulturemia of certain aggressors can make the average art lover among us appear anemic. I suspect that most of us are more like Stendhal's protagonist Fabrice, in *The Charterhouse of Parma*, than we are like Stendhal himself (assuming we believe the notoriously unreliable author's account); Fabrice wanders around in confusion during the Battle of Waterloo, wondering, again and again, if he's been in "a real battle," if he is participating in history. I have often wandered around museums in a similar state, sidling up to various canvases, asking myself: Am I being sufficiently moved? Am I having a genuine experience of art? The vandal who cuts or kisses a canvas seems to have no doubt.

Or what if what I'm really admiring when I look at art is money? Everybody knows that art can be worth a tremendous amount of it—that the rich park their surplus cash in one artwork or another, that even artists interested in "dematerialization" usually produce souvenirs of their performances that can be sold by galleries. But we tend to deny prioritizing art's economic value; we say we appreciate it for its beauty, for its conceptual power, whatever. These things are not always mutually exclusive, of course, and many people are explicit that art is a business (Warhol: "Good business is the best art"). But unlike most businesses, the art world typically asserts that art is first and foremost something other than a commodity.

There is a rationality to disavowing economic interest, in part because such disavowal leads to the accumulation of what the sociologist Pierre Bourdieu called "symbolic capital"—prestige, authority, an aura of purity and authenticity—which actually helps you sell your product. It's perhaps easier to imagine denying that art is a commodity when talking about a Rembrandt or a Rothko than when talking about a Warhol print of a dollar sign or a Jeff Koons balloon dog.

But I would argue that much, if by no means all, of contemporary art since Warhol assumes a posture of monetary disinterestedness, one based on criticism of the market itself. Walk through the galleries of New York's Chelsea or Lower East Side and you will find works that claim to be a critique of capitalism or the commodification of art: recontextualized porn that attacks the capitalist spectacularization of sex, sculptures made of a devalued currency, and so on. Such art might be brilliant, or disturbing, or derivative and predictable; regardless, it is very much for sale.

Duchamp considered anything art so long as it was branded by the artist's signature. (Indeed, Duchamp—in a gesture Umanets might have had in mind—once signed someone else's mural at the Café des Artistes and then declared it one of his ready-mades; though destroyed, it's sometimes listed among his works.) Scores of artists since have, like Metzger, seen their art as "an attack ... on art dealers and collectors who manipulate modern art for profit." But a profit can be made by selling attacks on profit because they earn dealers and collectors more symbolic capital, allow them to appear above the monetary. As long as the "attack" can be repackaged as salable, it's art. "Vandalism" is the word assigned to those destructive acts that the art world can't profit from. (The most startling aspect of Umanets's naïveté is his failure to understand the difference in value between his signature and the signature of an art-world celebrity.) Vandalism speaks—or spits on, kisses, slashes—the open secret of economic interest.

This is why vandalism that *increases* dollar value isn't vandalism. In 1964, Dorothy Podber—a self-described witch and performance artist who had worked at the Nonagon Gallery in Manhattan—visited Andy Warhol's Factory. Podber asked whether she could "shoot" a stack of his Marilyn paintings. Warhol, apparently believing she meant to photograph the paintings, consented. Podber then removed a pistol and fired at the stack, damaging several canvases.

Podber doesn't warrant mention as a vandal in Gamboni's survey, or in the ever-expanding Wikipedia page on art vandalism (maybe I'll add her), or in any of the compilations of acts of vandalism I've seen in the wake of Umanets. Surely she would have made these lists if Warhol had called the cops; instead, after politely asking Podber not to shoot his work again, he simply renamed the canvases: *Orange*

Marilyn became *Shot Orange Marilyn*, *Red Marilyn* became *Shot Red Marilyn*, and so on. Because, and only because, Warhol underwrote the Shot Marilyns, vandalism never occurred. Warhol was the more powerful witch; he made Podber disappear. She gets credit neither as a vandal nor as an artist. In 1989, *Shot Red Marilyn* sold for $4 million, at that time a record for a Warhol at auction.

When Dinos Chapman was asked to explain how his defacing and displaying Goya's *Los Caprichos* etchings was legitimate art, not vandalism, he said: "You can't vandalize something by making it more expensive" (the Chapman brothers' "revised and improved" versions of *Los Caprichos* were selling in 2005 at London's White Cube gallery for $26,000 apiece). Remember that this was part of Umanets's and Pinoncelli's defense—that they were actually increasing the value of the works in question. They are vandals in part because they got the economics wrong in a way that makes the economics plain.

Following Umanets's attack, there were, understandably, calls for silence: don't give the idiot the satisfaction of fame, which will just inspire more vandals; under no circumstances treat him like an artist. (Who knows how many acts of vandalism are never reported by museums? They have an interest in keeping lenders and insurers from thinking of works in their possession as vulnerable to attack.) The desire to strike the name of the vandal from the record has a long history. In 356 BC, Herostratus burned down the Temple of Artemis at Ephesus with the primary motivation of making himself famous. To prevent copycat acts of vandalism by those seeking immortality, the authorities not only executed the arsonist but, under pain of death, forbade the mention of his name. Needless to say, it didn't work; Theopompus recorded the event in his *Hellenics*.

I have no interest in promoting a contemporary Herostratus, in making celebrities out of Umanets and similar figures. But if we ultimately believe a vandal is a vandal and not an artist because he devalues someone else's property, then art-world radicalism doesn't look very radical at all. If we believe it's vandalism because it destroys a thing of beauty as opposed to creating more of it, then many vanguard artists who employ destruction need to be reclassified. The vandal haunts the artist, the art lover, and the art institution because he dramatically acts on what we say but do not mean.

It just so happens that the Tate Britain—a sister of the museum where Umanets attempted to reappropriate a Rothko—has an exhibition entitled Art Under Attack running through next month. It explores attacks on artworks from the Reformation to the present day; the Tate Britain's director, Penelope Curtis, told the *New York Times* that the show seems to be making the art world nervous. I was disappointed to learn that the damaged (or by now hopefully restored) Rothko isn't displayed, but the exhibition does include Metzger, Yoko Ono, and the Chapmans. It acknowledges some of the tenuousness and complexity of the distinction between art and vandalism; nevertheless, I suspect the exhibition is, in more than one sense, still guarded.

■

What would it mean to think beyond the economics of the art world, to move beyond both vandalism and the market it exposes? Is it possible to get outside the legacy of Duchamp—a legacy that has begotten, whatever Duchamp would have thought of them, Umanetses and Chapmans and Pinoncellis? In 2009, the Polish-born artist Elka Krajewska founded something she calls the Salvage Art Institute (SAI) in New York. The "institute" is basically Krajewska herself. She persuaded the AXA Art Insurance Corporation—one of the largest insurers of art in North America—to give her a sampling of their inventory of "total loss" art. When a work is damaged—in transit, in a fire or flood, in an act of vandalism—and an appraiser agrees with the owner of the work that it cannot be satisfactorily restored, or that the cost of restoration would exceed the value of the claim, the insurance company pays out the total value of the damaged work, which is then, legally speaking, worthless. I always assumed such artifacts were destroyed, but it turns out there are warehouses full of them; Krajewska visited one in Brooklyn. She now possesses more than forty objects that, as far as the art market is concerned, are no longer art.

The first public viewing of the SAI was held at the Arthur Ross Architecture Gallery, part of Columbia University's Graduate School of Architecture, last fall. Krajewska, collaborating with Mark Wasiuta, the school's director of exhibitions, mounted the damaged paintings on movable dollies and also displayed the (heavily redacted) paperwork that detailed the processing of the claims. Some of the damaged works were easily recognizable, such as a small Jeff Koons balloon dog lying in shards on a silver tray. (At Krajewska's exhibition, you can touch whatever you want; I admit I felt a frisson of transgression getting to handle the fractured sculpture, an icon I have wanted, in my more childish moments, to smash.)

The SAI explicitly positions itself as a kind of conceptual reversal of the Duchampian ready-made. Its mission statement reads:

> SAI conceives the declaration that an object is No Longer Art as the symmetrical inversion of the subjective declaration that any object may be art. The signature of the adjuster meets and cancels the signature of the artist.

And Krajewska preempts the possibility of these objects' being reappraised or resold:

> SAI seeks to maintain the zero-value of No Longer Art and recognizes its right to remain independent and divorced from the demands of future marketability.

I had my own experience of something like hyperkulturemia, a feeling of vertigo, when I visited the SAI. What moved me most were not those works that were clearly severely damaged—that had suffered some kind of violence—but those that appeared to me identical to their former incarnation as economically valuable art. For example, to my perhaps unsophisticated eye, several photographs—works by Anne Morgenstern, Rodney Smith, and even Henri Cartier-Bresson—seemed perfectly intact, despite what the owners and appraisers had decided. As I spent a few minutes holding each of these photographs in turn, I remembered the following anecdote from a book by the philosopher Giorgio Agamben:

> The Hasidim tell a story about the world to come that says everything there will be just as it is here. Just as our room is now, so it will be in the world to come; where our baby sleeps now, there too it will sleep in the other world. And the clothes we wear in this world, those too we will wear there. Everything will be as it is now, just a little different.

Several of the works in the SAI are just as they were, but a little different. We're all familiar with material things that take on a kind of magical power as a result of a signature: that's how branding functions in the gallery system and beyond, whether for Duchamp or Louis Vuitton. But it is incredibly rare to encounter the reversal of that process, to encounter an object freed from the market—freed without being shattered or spit on or torn. It was as if I could register as I held each of the photographs in my hands a subtle but momentous transfer of weight: the market's soul had fled; it was art outside of capitalism. Each work had been redeemed, both in the sense that the fetish had been converted back into cash, the claim paid out, but also in the more messianic sense of being saved from something, saved for something. For me these objects—just as they were, but a little different—were ready-mades for or from a world to come, a future where there is some other system of value, in the art world and beyond, than the tyranny of price. That's long been a dream of many artists and vandals alike.

Orhan Pamuk

Orhan Pamuk is a Turkish novelist; not only is he the country's bestselling author, he is also one of the preeminent novelists worldwide, winning the 2006 Nobel Prize in Literature. Since his debut with *Cevdet Bey and His Sons* (1982, still untranslated into English), he has written nine further novels, an autobiography, and a wide range of criticism, some of which was anthologized in 2007's *Other Colours*. As this title suggests, Pamuk has an eye sharply attuned to colors (consider other titles: *The White Castle* [1990], *The Black Book* [1994], *My Name is Red* [2001], *The Red-Haired Woman* [2016]) and to artworks more generally; after publishing his novel *The Museum of Innocence* in 2008, he curated an actual museum collection in an Istanbul house. The importance of art in Pamuk's writing is in part explained by this essay, in which he confesses to having dreamt of becoming a painter "between the ages of seven and 22," imagining art as "my path to happiness." Although he "wished [he] could forget" this dream, he admits that it "endured unsettlingly in some corner of my mind, like a sin." This aspiration towards visual artistry manifests more as self-consciousness than the jealousy of other writers (like Ben Lerner), but it is also productive—it leads him to question how different forms can learn from one another, "to look beyond what words represent and signify, and notice instead their texture and the connections they form."

When Orhan Pamuk Met Anselm Kiefer

I've always thought of art as my path to happiness. Between the ages of seven and 22, I wanted to be a painter, and spent a lot of time drawing, especially during my adolescence. My family were supportive. I even had a little studio in an apartment in Istanbul, full of old furniture. I had plans to be a famous painter one day.

Twenty years later, none of these dreams had come true; I was writing novels in Istanbul, and getting them published. Art still remained a promise of future happiness, rather than something I could enjoy in the present.

Throughout the 1980s, whenever I came across the work of great artists like Anselm Kiefer, I was seized by an emotion somewhere between jealousy and regret at having missed out on the life I was meant to live. But part of me understood that the happiness I yearned for was out of my reach. Kiefer's formidable art proved that, contrary to what I'd believed in my childhood and youth, thinking in images and daydreams was no guarantee of artistic fulfilment. The strength behind each vigorous stroke of the brush, and indeed the physical presence of the painter, were both essential components of that magical equation we call art. My body, my shoulder, my arm, my hand would not have been capable of creating any of this, and the force of Kiefer's art helped me a little to come to terms with this painful truth.

Still, the dream of emulating Kiefer, or at least the hope that I might yet be an accomplished painter someday, endured unsettlingly in some corner of my mind, like a sin I wished I could forget. This joyful restlessness was inspired in part by those elements of Kiefer's oeuvre that stand alongside his outsize, dramatic paintings: the books he created in his youth, with the help of photos, which have made him an artist so dear to writers and bibliophiles.

In Kiefer's aesthetics, books themselves are sacred, as well as the texts they carry. His art conveys this feeling by accentuating the "thingness"—to use Heidegger's term—of letters, words and texts. When we look at the enormous books he has sculpted in recent years from sheets of lead and other metals, they tell us that their sacred quality exists in their textures as much as it does in the texts within. All his books—whether they are made of paper, metal or plaster—have the ability to leave a writer such as myself with the illusion that it is not the text itself that makes a book sacred, but the texture.

It is almost as if Kiefer's books are telling us to look beyond what words represent and signify, and notice instead their texture and the connections they form. This is somewhat like looking at a wall and being struck by its overall feel rather than the individual bricks that compose it. (Kiefer likes to study walls and paint each brick individually, just as he is interested in brick factories, but when we observe his work, we don't necessarily see those bricks, or even the wall itself—rather, what we notice is its texture.) I wonder if this is the key to his brilliance; or perhaps it is because his paintings are so extraordinary that they give rise to these impressions.

One thing I'm sure of is that this literary texture percolates from Kiefer's books to the rest of his art. With every mountain, plain, forest, German legend and neglected railway track or road he depicts, this great artist invites us to read his paintings as if they were books. The literary texture that spills over from Kiefer's books and illuminates his paintings turns all that he creates into something we can read. We find ourselves looking at his trees, his railroads and mountains as if they were text; their secrets are hiding just beneath that vibrant, vivid, surprising surface we are reading, though reading it, of course, is not so easy after all.

My mind was busy with these thoughts as Kiefer's gallerist, Thaddaeus Ropac, took me to the artist's studio in France. In the car on the way out of Paris, I was nervous but equally excited, like a little boy going to the movies for the first time. I had met the artist in Salzburg in 2008, and I was familiar with his work from museums and books. Perhaps seeing his work inside his studio would bring forth new emotions. Perhaps one day I might even give up on novels and devote my time to painting.

There was so much to admire in that enormous studio that when I saw the artist's new work, I was overwhelmed. I knew Kiefer's world well; I had seen paintings like these before, and sculptures similar to the poppies and childlike airplanes that stood before me now. There was some comfort in seeing the artist's now familiar handwriting on his paintings. As ever, Kiefer had left written indications on his paintings that pointed us towards the legend, the text or the poet (Ingeborg Bachmann, Paul Celan, Arthur Rimbaud) that had inspired him in each case, and reminded us of the story or the history that lay behind each painting.

As I nervously paced around Kiefer's immense studio, intoxicated by what I saw, I found myself thinking once again that perhaps the reason why I loved these paintings so much was the artist's ability to demonstrate the kinship of words and images, legends and landscapes. All these words, letters, trees, mountains, frail flowers and forgotten roads were part of a single text, and shared a common texture. All I wanted was to be able to read these paintings and the forceful brushstrokes that had formed them. But I also knew that no matter how many times I looked back and forth between the words and the images before me, I would never be able to cross this horizon and find peace on the other side of that mountain on which I saw many signs and letters inscribed. That boundless tension between words and images, text and art, is at the heart of all Kiefer's oeuvre.

In the beginning was, indeed, the word, Kiefer's paintings seem to tell their beholder. But to look at art and the world and really understand what we see is so much more pleasurable than reading words and letters can ever be. Is it possible, then, to look at a painting and be able, ultimately, to read it? Is it possible to treat a book as a painting, and a painting as a book?

Texts and images all descend from an inexhaustible multitude of myths. Among the artists whose work I know, Kiefer is perhaps the most talented, ambitious and literary of them all, and maybe that is why his universe appeals to me so strongly.

As I stood before the masterpieces in his enormous studio, the child in my heart kept telling me that I could still be a painter—that I, too, could reveal the realm inside my mind through art. On the other hand, my grownup self, the happy, satisfied writer, was trying to remind myself that I was already doing with novels what Kiefer did in his art, and that I should be more humble and realistic in my expectations. Yet, dazed by the beauty of the paintings around me, I grieved over the loss of the childhood dream of painting I'd left behind.

That evening, Ropac hosted a dinner in his home on the banks of the Seine. He sat Kiefer and me next to each other before turning to the assembled guests to announce: "One of them wanted to be a writer and became a painter. The other wanted to be a painter and became a writer." We all laughed. But in truth, for me there was nothing to laugh about, since I still felt this way. Was that why I was getting through so much white wine? The waiters in their white gloves never let my glass sit empty.

Soon, I felt light-headed, and I began to think of the diary-notebook I kept in my pocket. It contained a number of little drawings I'd made with great care and fervor. Should I show the best of them to the great artist sitting next to me? He would surely understand.

I could feel, though, that this would be inappropriate. Everyone would laugh at me. I'd look ridiculous, like the dignified soldier in Thomas Mann's *Tonio Kröger* who stands up in the middle of a crowded formal dinner to recite his poetry. Perhaps I could show Anselm my drawings in some quiet corner later on. He was kind and understanding, and he would certainly treat my artistic instincts with respect.

But there was a firmer, more pragmatic whisper in my mind telling me: what's the point? If you really must draw, do it in the privacy of your own home, where no one can see. Don't go seeking anyone's approval—least of all a famous painter.

The whole thing was such a delicate matter for me that I resented the other guests' enjoyment as they made small talk around the table. Anselm was talking to them, too, taking in all the delights life had to offer to a man who had managed to achieve even more than what he'd hoped for. For a moment, I felt completely alone. I joined in the conversation. I decided I must never show him my drawings. Yet I still felt the impulse to put my hand in my jacket pocket and bring out my notebook.

Then, Kiefer turned to me. He looked shy, almost uncertain.

"I have written a book, you know," he said. "I would like you to read it."

"What's it called? Who publishes it?"

"*Notizbücher*. But there is no English translation."

There followed a long silence. I felt I liked Kiefer even more, now. He wasn't just a great artist; he was profound. It was a good thing I hadn't bothered him with my drawings. Not to mention that, for the first time in my life, I felt at peace with the fact that I would never be a painter.

The dinner did not last long, and the guests suddenly got lost in the Parisian night. Outside, it was rainy and windy. I was agitated. I wanted to walk along the Seine, sort out my thoughts, and think about the day I'd spent in Kiefer's studio. The beautiful paintings I had seen, the mythical, literary landscapes, came back to me now like memories from my own past. I wondered what there could be in his book, the one he wrote. But all that came to mind were his extraordinary paintings, and occasionally—as we all do when we admire someone—I felt as if I had painted them.

Ali Smith

Ali Smith is a Scottish writer. The author of ten novels and five collections of short stories, she began her career as a copywriter and fiction reviewer, before the publication of her debut short story collection in 1995. Smith continues to write prolifically for the *Guardian* and the *Times Literary Supplement*. Her "Seasons Quartet" of novels, which sought to respond directly to the political conditions of the UK following Brexit, began with 2016's *Autumn* and concluded with 2020's *Spring*. This series has elevated Smith to the status of major cultural critic, with many reviewers drawing attention to the speed of the series' writing and publication. Smith herself noted that she wanted to experiment with "how closely to contemporaneousness a finished book might be able to be in the world, and yet how it could also be, all through, very much about stratified, cyclic time," drawing links between the immediacy of the essay and its function as cultural criticism, and her ambitions for the series. Smith's frequently experimental approach to form is characteristically connected to time in this way—exemplified by her 2014 novel *How to be Both*, but manifested in this essay, too, where her clipped sentences and abrupt style ("Her talent? Simultaneous is a good word for it.") reflect her own central observation about Sonia Delaunay's work. Delaunay's art creates the effect, Smith argues, that "thinking and the artistic act of representation are both visible, reverberating, physical energies."

We Must Not Be Isolated

Her 1916 self-portrait? It's a smiling refutation of the figurative. Or, rather, a refutation of *just* being figurative. It's a work that's a portrait of herself *and* a portrait of the interplay between the figurative and the abstract, as if that's what the self is anyway, color slabs, curves and shapes, and a smile beneath an eye that's at once a wink and wide open, a head that radiates color either as a gorgeous multi-resonant hat, or as if thinking and the artistic act of representation are both visible, reverberating, physical energies. All of the above, simultaneously.

Her talent? Simultaneous is a good word for it (the favored Delaunay word for what both Sonia and her husband Robert did, *simultané*)—a state of being or a happening or a union of several things at the same time. Plus, she removed (or made invisible, or revealed as an unreality) the dividing lines not just between the colors that make a painting but between art forms and all forms: art and fashion, design, business, art and life itself; instead, she revealed and emphasized the natural and aesthetic interconnections between them. Her transformations changed and united the worlds of design, décor, fashion, always gesturing to, changing and uniting all the divided things throughout the world itself. There was nothing her color-vision excluded, from poetry, books and book bindings to lampshades, cushions, accessories; from clothes and fabrics to furniture, shops, casinos, opera, ballet, theatre, cinema—at one point, even the transformation of a Jesuit chapel was on the cards. And then there were the cards themselves (the playing cards, I mean), and the alphabet, and a couple of iconic automobiles—and, over and above this, the renewing transformation that all of this wrought in the people who wore the clothes, who used the fabrics, who saw the colors.

Somewhere in all of this, and equally part of her discipline, is the implication of a questioning of any false line dividing the union and simultaneity of the inner and outer self. In her written self-portrait, the short memoir published in 1978, *Nous irons jusqu'au soleil* (We

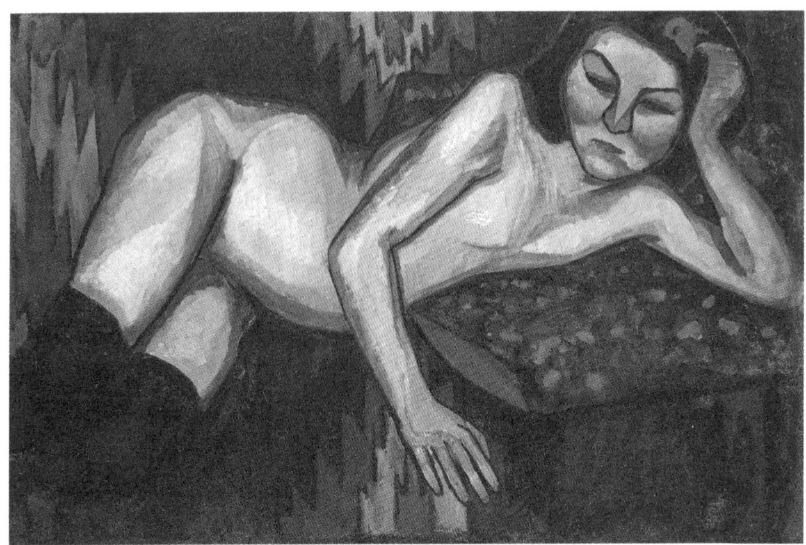

Sonia Delaunay, "Nu Jaune (Yellow Nude)," 1908, oil on canvas.
Courtesy of the Musée des Beaux-Arts de Nantes.

Will Go Right Up to the Sun), she remembers (in a vibrant present tense) the time of making her first collages, discovering her urge to paint and cover things with color—a box, cushions, waistcoats, coats and dresses—and how these first "simultaneous objects" worked to "astonish our Sunday visitors . . . it's just that I see colour contrasts everywhere in life . . . I do it all for the fun of it. . . . Colour excites me. It's not that I'm thinking about what I'm doing. These things come from inside, gut-level." Then she adds—both prophetically and because it's already known, because she's in her 90s when she writes this book, and because something about that word *simultané* means that past, future and present tenses are all held together too—"It's going to be the same all my life."[1]

Half a century before (or 15 years later, or all at once), in 1926, she's giving a lecture at the Sorbonne where she marks out the path of a brand new and, as yet, unrecognized canon, one that leads through the great modern French experimental painters of the past decades directly to fabric design and haute couture via a new and vitally collaborative relationship between the arts and design. Back in 1904, when she's still Sonia Terk, in her late teens, she's holding forth passionately in her diary: "We must not be isolated. Peoples should aim to unite, to amalgamate, they should not isolate themselves."[2] Partly, she's writing this in response to her own Jewishness and her teenage reading about, and close knowledge of, the sufferings of the Jewish people in Ukraine and Russia, where she's grown up. (Born into poverty as Sara Stern in Odessa in 1885, she spent the years after her early childhood in St. Petersburg with an aunt and uncle who adopted her into a lifestyle much more luxurious than that of her parents.) By the time she gets to Paris in her early 20s, she is highly educated, incredibly well-read, free-thinking, fluent in several languages, well-traveled in the world and already on the way—highly unconventional though it is for any young woman at the time—to being a painter. Partly, this ethos of connectivity, of amalgamation, is the truest self-portrait of Delaunay there is. Love of the ever-connectivity of all things, especially in the contrasts between things, runs through her life, her work and her writing.

It was the heart of her marriage. "I was born the same year as Robert Delaunay, under the same sun, some three thousand versts away," she wrote in *Nous irons jusqu'au soleil*.[3] Simultaneous distance and co-existence. "Our lives became tied together. The passion of painting was our principle bond."[4] Photographs of the couple spill over with a multitude of friends, a mix of poets, artists, dancers and choreographers with whom they didn't just co-exist, they made collaborative works. Her multiglot talents meant that she was, for this group, everything from a natural bridger of national differences and languages to an aesthetic conduit (for instance, her translating of Wassily Kandinsky's pre-war prose and articles); borderlessness was her natural state and Delaunay's sociability and hospitality were legendary. So, too, was the great energy and happiness that came simply from being anywhere near the simultaneity of art and environment the Delaunays called home. As one lightstruck, lovestruck young surrealist writer, René Crevel, put it: "After five minutes in Sonia Delaunay's house, who has not been surprised to find in himself more conviction, more hope, even happiness?"[5]

Naturally, just as the cut and look of her clothes always enhanced the individuality of the wearer, this working together with others always miraculously revealed or enhanced her aesthetic individuality. She was fierce and bristling in her protection of the equality, the connection and the simultaneous separateness of her relationship with

Robert. A 1970s interview in *Art Talk* by the American art historian Cindy Nemser is revealing. Nemser asks Sonia about their togetherness in the invention of Orphism and color simultaneity. Nemser suggests that, according to what she's gathered from other commentators, in their collaboration, Sonia was the true force. Delaunay takes against Nemser's line of questioning. "You are speaking like somebody who writes about artists," she says at one point and then laughs, and you can tell how sharp she could be with people, how unsettling and tough, what an unsufferer of fools. She rises up like a high-hackled cat: "We were two moving forces. One made one thing and one made the other. . . . I made my paintings alone."

In the individual act of the work, her desire was always to reveal a reality of non-division, a natural and unified assemblage. "I want to create a finished painting," she said towards the end of her life, "a painting that is not fragmented . . . it won't be possible to see where [the colors] pass from one to another."[6]

In her very earliest paintings, influences from Paul Gauguin, Vincent van Gogh and the Fauves lightly mask her strongest instinct: an argument between color and line that's so insistent it's almost vocal. The many mask-like faces, the figures in physical separation from their backgrounds, as if superimposed on their environments and disagreeing with its and their own saturation, display a kind of stunned intoxication at their depth of color and its remarkable depth all round them.

Her painting *Nu Jaune* (Yellow Nude, 1908) is a vision of a woman made, changed and trapped by line while the power of color goes on all around her, even through her. Her body seems dipped, tempered at the line by color itself and by a different possibility, when it comes to line, than the black outline that contains her: it's as if she's trailing her hand in the impact made by this argument of color and line and something about this existence is a drag—no, worse, it's a louche prison, a prostitution. This is a picture where a black line represents a closing of the eyes. Meanwhile, all round her, the fabric of things offers something different, even possibly luxurious; the only untrammeled richness or ease in the picture comes in the shape of the cushion, free of outline, inside which the use of color itself is free of outline; it's so free that some of that color is leaching up out of the object and has even reached, on its own terms, the nude's hair and her head.

The real breakthrough came when forms themselves—things unused to being understood simultaneously—came together for Delaunay. In 1911, she made a cradle cover for her and Robert's baby, Charles. "When it was finished, the arrangement of the pieces of material seemed to me to evoke cubist conceptions and we then tried to apply the same process to other objects and paintings."[7] It's a shape made of shapes. It's a work of (and for) practical comfort, brought together from fragments and scraps. Its reds are still vibrant a hundred years later and the surprise of it is that its remnant state is itself a sort of textural unexpected pleasure, as if she's tapped an untapped joy—that a single thing made of so many disparate things is in itself a joy, with its so many irregular pieces, shapes, colors and textures patiently stitched into a larger irregularity. It is an act of love.

For Delaunay, the effect of such a window on the world was a resonant aesthetic liberation. "Little by little, the apartment was transformed: the walls were painted white and the lampshades and cushions dressed in a mosaic of paper and fabric. I rebound books that I loved ... in the manner of an assemblage ... the assemblage of bits of fabric gave birth to a unique style, according to which I executed a portrait of Nijinsky dancing."[8]

The dancer was up and kicking: it was only two years till Delaunay would paint the first and most dancey of her masterpieces of simultaneity. *Le Bal Bullier* (1913) is a painting in which the play between abstract and figurative is just that: sheer playfulness. It demonstrates a back-and-forth embrace, so that the whole painting, the whole long room, seems to be dancing in a revelation of love and connection. (It reminds me of a scene in a Max Linder silent film—the title has escaped me—in which a couple are so in love that when they start dancing to piano music, soon the pictures, the table, the furniture and even the piano itself can't help but dance too.) More: this painting has a new and spatial sense of narrative, a sequential shift that simultaneously denies a fixed sequence. Eye-wise, we're pulled along it in both directions, and this makes us part of its dance of shifting perspectives. It's painted on mattress ticking, so the dance/painting is also in some ways a bed, a love act of figurative/abstract symbiosis, in which everything is movement, everything an inner and outer dancing.

"Abstract and sensual have to marry, for me," Delaunay wrote in

Nous irons jusqu'au soleil. Her second version of *Le Bal Bullier* is a much more abstracted affair, colors seen as an elemental blur in a dance so vital and swirling that shape has become nothing but color. Both paintings were named for the dance hall at which she, Robert and their friends would strut their stuff (two francs entry on Thursday nights and half price on Saturdays), usually dressed in Sonia's early simultaneous clothes, bright swirls of patched color-amalgam, which gave them the visible status of glorious jesters, surreal panacheful dandies.

Guillaume Apollinaire's description of these clothes—their fusion of "woollen cloth, taffeta, tulle, flannelette, watered silk and *peau de soie*," the "purple dress, wide purple-and-green belt and, under the jacket, a corsage divided into brightly coloured zones, delicate or faded, where the following colours are mixed: antique rose, yellow-orange, Nattier blue, scarlet, etc."[9]—sounds remarkably like what the American poet Wallace Stevens longed for in his "Disillusionment of Ten O'Clock" (1915). It's a poem disappointed by dull houses "haunted by white nightgowns," none "green, / Or purple with green rings, / Or green with yellow rings, / Or yellow with blue rings," a sure sign that the imagination has lost its mojo, that nothing is properly intoxicating, that the necessary Strangeness that makes life vibrant has left life.

Delaunay herself was a lover and understander of poets, drawn to them especially when it came to the possibilities of fruitful collaboration. "Poetry of words / poetry of colours" she wrote, "poetry moves / through all / the creations of art."[10] "A poet" was one of her favorite things to call her husband, who worked with colors rather than words and, over the years, she made a work to accompany writings by Stéphane Mallarmé and Arthur Rimbaud. Apollinaire, who liked a bit of indivision between the graphic and the poetic himself, was one of the Delaunays' earliest friends and one of Robert's most important explainers and critical supporters. Above all, Sonia was taken with the work of the Swiss-born novelist and poet Blaise Cendrars, and their collaboration produced, in *La prose du Transsibérien et de la Petite Jehanne de France* (Prose of the Trans-Siberian and of Little Jehanne of France, 1913), the first-ever artist's book, an extraordinary unfolding creation that is longer than a human being. Her part of it all was "an improvisation, an impression" of Cendrars's long text about a journey (real? imaginary?) taken with his young prostitute lover from Moscow to Harbin in Mongolia.

It is a simultaneous fall and rise of color and shape. Colors bleed across the images, so they're never really divided from the text. A blue skyscape, greenery and shafts of sun seem to break over and flash through the colored blocks of text as they would through the moving windows of a train. The eye has to travel the poem; in fact, the eye animates the work in all directions. At its end, down at the foot (or is it its start? because the work, like *Le Bal Bullier*, is a spatial narrative, at once centrifugal and centripetal) is one of Delaunay's renderings of the Eiffel Tower, round which she always slings a ring, as if she's won the tower in a game of hoop-la or, in a making of a sensual male-female fusion of symbols, as if the Eiffel tower is always reaching up to pair with the sun.

The tower was a favorite symbol Sonia shared with Robert; he was excited by the idea that the number of copies of *La prose du Transsibérien et de la Petite Jehanne de France* they planned to publish would, unfolded and placed end to end, be as tall as the actual tower. For Sonia, the tower turns up again and again: early on, she spelled her name on her letterhead as "DelAunay." She is good, too, at suggesting the endless surprise of an "o" or an "o," as an eye, a target, a breast or, simply, a resonant, concentric shape; I see her circling Os as a complete modernist makeover of the renaissance halo. Later in her work and life, her use of the "s" shape promises the continuance of a road or path. The cover of her colorful book *Alphabet* (1972) suggests that the letters themselves are emanations both of color and of each other: the A B C D E and F rise out of each other like family, in a sharing and displaying of colors that happen to take on such meaningful shapes.

Everything is more than itself—as in *Prisme électriques* (Electric Prisms), her large painting from 1913, which revisits the power of *La prose du Transsibérien et de la Petite Jehanne de France*. A reference to it, relatively very small, can be seen to the left of two huge multicolored discs, forms from which energy radiates in a revelation of curving interconnectivity; it is as if the painting is asking whether the book, which was made a year earlier, is only an incidental part of such a huge reverberation or is the source of such vivid power, such rhythmic emanation. Or both.

Cendrars wrote about Delaunay's dresses as if they made women into works of art: "on the hip / the poet's signature." In turn, Delaunay covered things and people with words as well as colors, designing dress-poems or poem-dresses including one for her friend the surrealist Tristan Tzara. She wrote that her costumes—for instance, at the Hotel Claridge ball in 1924—"surprised people. Ball gowns? Theatrical disguises? Paradoxes in painted silk ... I wanted, along with having fun, to show the many riches of women's lines and body movements.... It pleased me ... to watch a whole new creature appear."[11] Cendrars thought her colors, as well as being a kind of poetry, sang. It's always struck me as utterly natural that Charles, the Delaunays' son, grew up to be a great jazz critic and the friend and biographer of Django Reinhardt and his Quintette du Hot Club de France; they made music that sounds as if it were born, fully formed, from one of Sonia's images. Listen to Reinhardt's "Improvisation no. 2" (1938), a work of spatial gestures and linear curves, and you can glimpse what one of her paintings might imaginatively sound like.

Delaunay went to many concerts with her aficionado son and thought Louis Armstrong's music was "absolutely abstract." She titled one of her hundreds of fabric designs "Jazz"; she shares with the music an endless rhythmic inventiveness, which celebrates the connections between opposites—waves and fractals, angles and curves, fabric and life, nature and artifice. It's a celebration, too, of the energy of a repeating pattern that is, paradoxically, never subsumed by sameness.

Her fabric designs, along with her clothing and interior design work, kept the world from the door, regardless of the vicissitudes of history. (She avoided financial ruin despite the Russian Revolution, the Wall Street Crash and two world wars.) But the fact that design was an integral part of her art and her life is obvious from a photograph of her taken in 1923: she's at her desk painting a pattern that seems to have leapt off the paper, onto her clothes and into the skein of fabric next to her. "Contemporary fashion," she said in the early 1930s, "ought to start from two principles: vital, unconscious, visual sensuality on the one hand, and the craft of fabrication on the other ... as if everything begins anew every day."[12]

This newness she repeatedly defines as a liberated language—a whole new kind of poetry, and a uniter of the arts. "The theatre of colour must be composed like a verse of Mallarmé, like a page of Joyce: perfect and pure juxtaposition, exact sequences, each element apportioned its correct weight with absolute rigour," she wrote. But there is immense freedom from any fixed or received meaning in this new language of color. "Beauty refuses the constraint of meaning or description."[13] In it, too, there's a steadiness which suggests that every system or machine, even those apocalyptic ones roaring in the 1930s towards Nazism and the foul rot of World War II, can be seen as she sees the airplanes she painted for the French Palais del'Air—for the 1937 Paris *Exposition* dedicated to Art and Technology in Modern Life—as just color, color and more color. Somehow, this is heartening, liberating, rather than naïve. The darker palette in her painting after Robert's death in 1941 of cancer, and in the work she made during the war in the occupied south of France—living from month to month between fears and losses, and with a stack of artillery shells under her hotel window—reveals the colors themselves as all the brighter.

They've stayed fresh. Simultaneity doesn't just conjure a constant present or confirm a continual, always colorful state against all the odds—it also gestures toward canceling the timeline altogether. More than 60 years after Delaunay made her son a cradle cover, the French singer/songwriter Françoise Hardy, the epitome of the new and the young, was photographed wearing a dress based on a Delaunay design. Half a century further down the line, I'm standing in front of *Electric Prisms* at Tate Modern, marveling at how a picture can lead a thinking human being to breathe more fully, and a child runs past me in delight, speeding from room to room in trainers that are flashing with irregular, multi-colored electric lights.

"It is more simple than people make it," the aging Delaunay told that annoying interviewer in the 1970s, who had just pronounced her work "a kind of force, a universal force, a kind of energy of light and colour." Delaunay shook off the implications. "Children like me. It is a big compliment."

Be pinned down and defined? Outlined? Fixed? Told we're one thing rather than another? The fabric of things, and of us, is much richer via the wide-open, simultaneously winking eye of Sonia Delaunay.

Notes

1. Sonia Delaunay, *Nous irons jusqu'au soleil*, trans. Ali Smith (Paris: Editions Robert Laffont), 1978.
2. *Sonia Delaunay* (London: Tate Gallery Publishing, 2014), 20.
3. Delaunay, *Nous irons*, 3.
4. *The New Art of Color: The Writings of Robert and Sonia Delaunay* (New York: Viking Press, 1978), 165.
5. *The New Art of Color*, 169.
6. *Sonia Delaunay*, 3.
7. *The New Art of Color*, 210.
8. *The New Art of Color*, 210–11.
9. *The New Art of Color*, 180.
10. *The New Art of Color*, 213.
11. Delaunay, *Nous irons*, 93.
12. *The New Art of Color*, 208.
13. *The New Art of Color*, 212.

Zadie Smith

Zadie Smith is a novelist and one of the foremost contemporary essayists. In spite of her early suspicion of novelists who turn to essays, the author (who, in the title of her 2009 collection of essays, freely admits to *Changing My Mind*) has gone on to publish regular essays for the *Guardian*, the *New York Review of Books*, and the *New Yorker* (among others), and has released two further collections (2018's *Feel Free* and 2020's *Intimations*) to complement her five novels. Smith is a fascinating essayist in part because she consistently works from a position of intellectual modesty. In the forward to *Feel Free*, Smith herself noted that "essays about one person's affective experience have, by their very nature, not a leg to stand on . . . all they have is their freedom." And yet she is also the essayist who can write a line like this: "a line of argument that might lead you to believe Clement Greenberg is still busy over at *Commentary* instead of being dead for more than two decades." A line so flippant that even while it signals her insider knowledge, it undermines this kind of insider approach. With this essay, Smith marks herself out as having a particularly commanding perspective on Black British painting; in others, Smith ventriloquizes Billie Holiday in the forward to a book of photographs of the singer, *Billie Holiday at Sugar Hill* (2017), utilizing fiction to comment on art. Content, after all, as Lynette Yiadom-Boakye, the subject of Smith's essay, reflects, finds its own form.

Lynette Yiadom-Boakye's Imaginary Portraits

The exhibition space on the fourth floor of the New Museum, in New York, is a long room with a high ceiling. You might expect towering video screens in here, or something bulky and three-dimensional, requiring circling—entering, even. But on a recent day the room was filled with oils. The show has a melancholy, literary title, "Under-Song For A Cipher," and consists of seventeen paintings hung low, depicting a set of striking individuals, all slightly larger than human scale, though not imposingly so. Most are on herringbone linen; one is on canvas. It's impossible to avoid noticing that they are all—every man and each woman—physically beautiful. Mostly they are alone. They sit, stretch, lounge, stand, and are often lost in contemplation, their eyes averted. If they are with others, the company is never mixed, as if too much heat might be generated by introducing that half-naked man over there to this sharp-eyed dancing girl.

In the oeuvre of the British-Ghanaian painter Lynette Yiadom-Boakye, there are quite a few dancers, lithe in their leotards, but all of her people look as though they might well belong to that profession. They are uniformly elegant. One young man puts his hands on his knees and laughs, with his legs apart and his feet turned out; he is dressed simply, like the rest, in blocks of swiftly laid paint, creating here a black vest, there some white trousers. No shoes. The artist dislikes attaching her figures to a particular historical moment, and there's no way around the historicity of shoes. Sometimes the men hold animals like familiars—an owl, a songbird, a cat. The colors are generally muted: greens and grays and blacks and an extraordinary variety of browns. Amid this sober coloration splashes of yellow and pink abound, and vivid blues and emerald greens, all tempered by the many snowdrop gaps of unpainted canvas, like floral accents in an English garden.

The surrounding walls are painted a dark heritage red, bringing to mind national galleries and private libraries, but also, for this viewer,

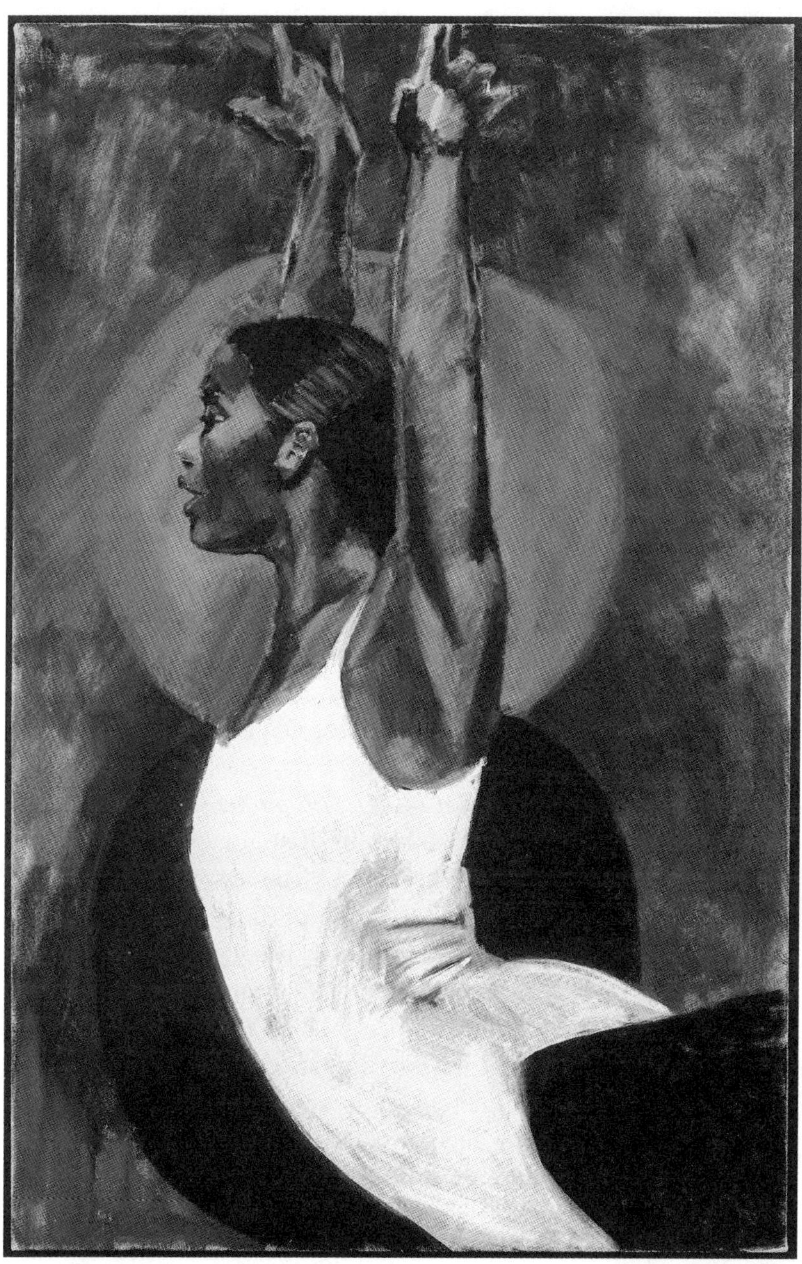

Lynette Yiadom-Boakye, "Light Of The Lit Wick," 2017, oil on linen, 79 x 51⅜ inches. © Lynette Yiadom-Boakye. Courtesy of the artist, Jack Shainman Gallery, New York and Corvi-Mora, London. Photograph by Marcus Leith.

the books you might find in such places, specifically the calico covers of nineteenth-century novels. This red has the effect of bringing a diverse selection of souls together, framing and containing them, much like a novel contains its people, which is to say, only partially. For Yiadom-Boakye's people push themselves forward, into the imagination—as literary characters do—surely, in part, because these are not really portraits. They have no models, no sitters. They are character studies of people who don't exist.

In many of Yiadom-Boakye's interviews, she is asked about the source of her images, and she tends to answer as a novelist would, citing a potent mix of found images, memory, sheer imagination, and spontaneous painterly improvisation (most of her canvases are, famously, completed in a single day). From a novelist's point of view, both the speed and the clarity are humbling. Subtleties of human personality it might take thousands of words to establish are here articulated by way of a few confident brushstrokes. But the deeper beguilement is how she manages to create the effect of wholly realized figures while simultaneously confounding so many of our assumptions about the figurative. The type of questions prompted by, say, Holbein (*What kind of a man was Sir Thomas More?*) or Gainsborough (*What was the social status of Mr. and Mrs. Andrews?*), or when considering a Lucian Freud (*What is the relation between painter and model?*), are all short-circuited here, replaced by an existential query not much heard in contemporary art: Who *is* this? The answer is both literal and liberating: No one. Nor will the titles of these paintings identify them. A dancing girl in the midst of an arabesque bears the caption "Light Of The Lit Wick." A gentleman in an orange turtleneck with a cat on his shoulder: "In Lieu Of Keen Virtue." That antic fellow with his hands on his knees: "A Cage For The Love." We have become used to titles that ironize or undercut what we are looking at, providing conceptual scaffolding for feeble visual ideas, or weak punch lines to duller jokes. For Yiadom-Boakye, titles are allusive; they should be considered, she has said, simply "an extra mark in the paintings." For an artist, she is unusual in describing herself as a writer as much as a painter—her short stories and prosy poems frequently appear in her catalogues. In a recent interview in *Time Out*, she reflected on the relation between these twin roles. "I don't paint about the writing or write about the painting," she said. "It's just the opposite, in fact:

I write about the things I can't paint and paint the things I can't write about." Her titles run parallel to the images, and—like the human figures they have chosen not to describe or explain—radiate an uncanny self-containment and serenity. The canvas is the text.

■

Given the self-confidence of this work, it's strange to note the anxiety that Yiadom-Boakye provokes in some critics. In the catalogue that accompanies the New Museum show, there is an essay by the academic art critic Robert Storr in which he deems it necessary to defend the work against the perceived retrogression of figurative painting: "If you accept Greenbergian premises and methodologies, representation was definitively eclipsed by abstraction sometime in the early 1950s"—a line of argument that might lead you to believe Clement Greenberg is still busy over at *Commentary* instead of being dead for more than two decades. The mid-century debate over the figurative and the abstract—which Greenberg's coining of the term "post-painterly abstraction" did much to further—aligned the figurative with illusion: the illusion of depth in a canvas, and the pretense of three-dimensional human life on what was, in truth, an inert, two-dimensional surface. The figurative was fundamentally nostalgic; its subject matter was kitsch; it was too easily manipulated for the purposes of propaganda, both political and commercial. Sentimental scenes of human life were, after all, what the Nazis and the Stalinists had championed. They were what the admen of Madison Avenue utilized every day. Meanwhile, the abstract sought to continue, in the realm of the visual, the modernist critique of the self. But, even when a critic allows for the somewhat antique formulation of these arguments (as Storr goes on to do), there is still something about the vicarious emotion provoked by the figurative that must be explained away or excused.

And so, in the same essay, Yiadom-Boakye is cautiously framed as the kind of artist who depicts an extreme otherness: "The impact of her pictures is of encountering people 'we'—the general North American art audience—have never met, coming from a world with which 'we' are unfamiliar. One that we have no basis for generalizing about or projecting our fantasies onto." Yet the subjects of these paintings are not members of a recently discovered Indigenous tribe in Papua

New Guinea but, rather, many handsome Black men and women in unremarkable domestic settings.

There is a respectful caution in this kind of critique which, though undoubtedly well intended in theory, in practice throws a patronizing chill over such work. Yiadom-Boakye is doing more than exploring the supposedly uncharted territory of Black selfhood, or making—in that hackneyed phrase—the invisible visible. (Black selfhood has always existed and is not invisible to Black people.) Nor are these paintings solely concerned with inserting the Black figure into an overwhelmingly white canon. Such pat truisms have a limited utility, especially when we find them applied without alteration to artists as diverse as Chris Ofili, Kerry James Marshall, and Kehinde Wiley. Ofili, in a delicate written response to Yiadom-Boakye's work, passes over the familiar rusty argument of figuration versus abstraction, and attends instead to the intimate visual details: "The tightness of her bun. The size of his ear. She knew so much about so little of him. She said so little he heard so much." Exactly. Here are some paintings of he and she, him and her. They say little, explicitly, but you hear much.

There are a few moments when the paintings also seem to respond more or less directly to a generalized notion of the "white canon." An overly literal triptych, "Vigil For A Horseman," features three handsome men laid out—in three different art-historical poses—on a candy-striped divan, calling to mind a riot of similar loungers: the Rokeby Venus, the picnickers of "Le Déjeuner sur l'Herbe," Adam meeting the finger of God, a Modigliani nude. But these are the weaker moments in the show. The strongest paintings pursue an entirely different relation: not the narrow point-for-point argument between artist and art history but the essential, living communication between art work and viewer, a relationship that Yiadom-Boakye reminds us is indeed vicarious, voyeuristic, ambivalent, and fundamentally uncontrollable.

■

For even if you are intimately familiar with the various shades of brown on offer here—even if you've always known these particular broad noses, the specific kink of Afro hair, the blue and orange tints that rise up through very dark skin—you are still, as a viewer, entirely engaged in the practice of fantastical projection. The figures themselves are the basis for your fantasy, with their teasing, ambiguous titles, women dancing to unheard music, or peering through binoculars at objects unseen. They seem to have souls—that ultimate retrogressive term!—though by "soul" we need imply nothing more metaphysical here than the sum total of one person's affect in the mind of another. Having this experience of other people (or of fictional simulacra of people) is an annoyingly persistent habit of actual humans, no matter how many convincing theoretical arguments attempt to bracket and contain the impulse, to carefully unhook it from transcendental ideas, or simply to curse it by one of its many names: realism, humanism, naturalism, figuration. People will continue to look at people—to listen to them, read about them, or reach out and touch them—and on such flimsy sensory foundations spin their private fantasias. Art has many more complex pleasures and problems, to be sure, but still this consideration of "souls" should be counted among them.

And when I asked myself, inevitably, who these souls in the gallery were, I thought of a group of intensely creative people in a small community, living simply in poky garrets, watchful and sensitive, determined and focused. Sometimes when they were flush—having sold a painting or a story—they'd do something purely for aesthetic pleasure, like buy a candy-striped divan or an owl or travel to Cadiz. Early New York beatniks, maybe, or some forgotten, South London chapter of the Bloomsbury Group. Poets, writers, painters, dancers, dreamers, philosophers—and lovers of same.

This fantasy was certainly my own projection, but I could find its narrative roots in the muted, modernist color palette and the "timeless" clothes, which turn out to be not so timeless: during the early decades of the twentieth century, Vanessa Bell wore these simple shifts (and no shoes) and Duncan Grant painted both his daughter and his Jamaican lover, Patrick Nelson, in similar swift blocks of color, where shirt or blouse meets trousers or skirt in a single mussed line, without recourse to belts or buttons. Yiadom-Boakye often cites the unfashionable British painter Walter Sickert as an influence, and it is perhaps here that the congruence occurs: Virginia Woolf was also an admirer of Sickert, and published a monograph about him; Vanessa, her sister, illustrated the cover.

Born in 1860, and a member of the Camden Town Group, Sickert, like Yiadom-Boakye, was gifted at painting wet-on-wet (completing canvases quickly, to avoid having to break the "skin" of paint that had dried overnight), disliked painting from nature, and specialized in ambivalently posed figures in domestic settings, about whom one longs to tell stories. Certainly from Sickert (and Degas before him) Yiadom-Boakye has inherited a narrative compulsion, which has less to do with capturing the real than with provoking, in her audience, a desire to impose a story upon an image. Central to this novelistic practice is learning how to leave sufficient space, so as to give your audience room to elaborate. (Sickert, with his spooky and suggestive tableaux of Camden prostitutes, was so successful in doing this that he unwittingly planted the seeds of an outrageous fiction—that he was Jack the Ripper, a theory still alive today.)

Yet the keenness to ascribe to Black artists some generalized aim—such as the insertion of the Black figure into the white canon—renders banal their struggles with a particular canvas, and with the unique problem each art work poses. (For Yiadom-Boakye, the problem of a painting, she has said, begins with "a color, a composition, a gesture, a particular direction of the light. My starting points are usually formal ones.") It also risks flattening out individual conversations with tradition. Kerry James Marshall, for his recent show "Mastry," at the Metropolitan Museum of Art, included a marvelously eclectic and unexpected selection of pieces from the Met's permanent collection, a supplementary "show within a show," which had the effect of positioning Marshall's own "mastry" as both a confrontation with and a continuation of the familiar Western European mastery of such figures as Holbein and Ingres. But Marshall also took us on a journey down side roads more obscure and intimate, deep into the thickets of an artist's individual passions. Why, out of all the masterpieces in the Met, does a man pick out a certain Japanese woodblock print, or a bull-shaped boli from West Africa? These are the mysteries of personal sensibility, often obscure to critics but never less than essential to artists themselves.

■

Sometimes the process of making art is a conversation not so much with tradition as with the present moment. Born in 1977, Yiadom-Boakye was nineteen when an exhibition of works from the collection of Charles Saatchi, "Sensation," opened in London, at the Royal Academy. The show presented, among other excitements, Damien Hirst's shark, the Chapman brothers' polymorphously perverse child mannequins, and Sarah Lucas's mordant mattress with its cucumber penis. "Sensation" and its Young British Artists dominated the art conversation, enraptured the tabloids, and relegated British portraiture to the debased realm of one-note arguments and conceptual gimmicks. (The most famous portrait in "Sensation"—Marcus Harvey's "Myra," a re-creation of a notorious photo of the British child-murderer Myra Hindley, rendered in a child's handprints—sparked so much controversy that the show was almost shut down.) Even the good work was ill served by the central conceit of the show, which encouraged visitors to look "past" the paint to the supposed sensation of the manifest content (Chris Ofili's Madonna with elephant dung, Jenny Saville's "fat" female nudes). At the time, Yiadom-Boakye had just finished a dispiriting one-year foundation course at Central Saint Martins, the prestigious art school in London, where she'd discovered, as she explained in a 2013 interview with Naomi Beckwith, a curator at the Museum of Contemporary Art in Chicago, that the conversations about her chosen form revolved around "what painters should or shouldn't be doing, linked to what the art world was or wasn't doing/saying." Some relief came when she left London, to pursue a BA at Falmouth College of Arts, in Cornwall, where the discussion was broader, though no less stringent: "If you were going to paint, you had to have a bloody good reason to do it. There was shame involved."

By the time Yiadom-Boakye returned to London, to do an MFA at the Royal Academy, she had endured many lectures on the death and/or the irrelevance of painting, and her own practice came to reflect some of these debates. Some of her earlier work, by her own admission, uses narrative literally, with both image and title supporting each other tautologically. From the Beckwith interview: "Four black girls standing with headphones on plugged into the floor, basically taking instructions from the devil, and its title was: 'The Devil Made me do it.'... I hadn't really defined a style yet. Because I hadn't got to grips with painting yet, I ignored the actual power that painting could have; I didn't trust that paint could do anything."

In the early aughts, her work began to feature rather cartoonish figures, which perhaps owe something to George Condo's grotesques, and carry with them the strong sense of a young artist giving herself a deliberate handicap, or, to put it another way, a series of exploratory formal constraints. In these works, Blackness seems to be depicted from the outside and therefore appears—as Blackness is often seen, by others—under the sign of monstrosity. (A parallel example is Kerry James Marshall's "A Portrait of the Artist as a Shadow of His Former Self" (1980), in which the artist appears as a grinning, minstrelesque mask.) Asked, in an e-mail, about this earlier style, Yiadom-Boakye replied, "It must have been a reaction to a lot of what was said to me. Humor and horror made sense because that was how I felt. Often-times it really worked, other times it was hugely dissatisfying. I think that's why I got rid of so much of it as I went along. Over time I realized I needed to think less about the subject and more about the painting. So I began to think very seriously about colour, light and composition. The more I worked, the more I came to realise that the power was in the painting itself. My 'colour politics' took on a whole new meaning."

■

One of the most persistent misapprehensions that exists between artists and viewers—and writers and readers—concerns the relative weight of content and form. Just as, in the mind of a writer, individual novels will tend, privately, to be considered not "the one in which John kills Jane" or "the one in which Kwame gets married" but, rather, "the one with the semicolons" or "the one in which I realized the possibility of commas," so that which looks like figuration to a layman like me ("Isn't that a beautiful fellow with his owl?") is, for the artist, as much about paint itself—its various possibilities, moods and effects, limits and freedoms. In nonfigurative work, these technical preoccupations are perhaps easier to spot, but, whether a human figure can be discerned in the work or no, the same battles with color, light, composition, and tone apply. One way to track intellectual movements in the arts is to follow the rise and fall of content versus form (as Susan Sontag, in her essay "On Style," pointed out not long after Greenberg effected his great separation of the abstract from the figurative). Falsely separating the two—and then insisting on the elevation of one over the other—happens periodically, and often has the useful side effect of revitalizing the art practice of the time, repressing what has become overly familiar or championing the new or the previously ignored.

"Sensation" marked Britain's parochial, delayed response to thirty years of complex aesthetic theory (mostly French and American) that had privileged content (in the form of "the concept") over form, but it also fatally and impurely mixed these ideas with the careerism of the YBAs themselves, who contributed their own professional anxieties, dressed up in contempt. Portraiture came to be considered "content," and therefore a subject that could be exhausted, despite (or maybe because of) its long, exalted history. And, once it was deemed to be exhausted, the consensus was that only the most hubristic (or nostalgic) young British artist would dare attempt it. *What is she trying to prove? Who does she think she is—an Old Master?* If you were a student in art school at the time, these debates could sound as much personal as theoretical. Over the years, Yiadom-Boakye has responded in paint, but also in writing, though always obliquely, as she seems to respond to everything. Some of her stories and poems involve people, and many more involve animals, but all of them have the sly, wise tone of fable. In a typically Kafkaesque short prose poem, "Plans of the Night," she gives to an owl and a "Deeply Skeptical Pigeon" the role of artist and antagonist:

> It was possible to perform the feats for which he was famed
> During the Day.
> But for the Owl there was something Infinitely Preferable
> About the Night.
> The Owl had difficulty explaining this to other birds.

The same difficulty, I imagine, that a young, talented painter at Saint Martins in the late nineties might have had explaining her preference for portraiture:

> The Pigeon argued that the Owl's insistence on a Nocturnal
>   Routine
> Had more to do with Self-Mythologizing and
> By extension, Self-Aggrandisement
> Than any Practical Need.

But in fact the Owl has "his mind on other things." He is an owl obsessed with practice itself, which, in his case, involves the hunting of a mouse in the grass. But the Skeptical Pigeon won't let it go:

"This Mystery, it's not real you know.
You're as dull and predictable as the Rest of Us."

The Owl, silent, focuses on his prey. Meanwhile, the Pigeon continues to upbraid him for his unseemly ambition:

"How appropriate! Always sat a Bough or two higher than the Rest of Us, looking down on everyone as usual."...
"You think you're Special, that you have some Authority over the Night."

The Owl, no longer listening, readies himself to swoop and catch that mouse, but, when he finally does so, his wing smacks the Pigeon in his head, breaking his neck and killing him. Cold comfort—the mouse, who has witnessed it all, escapes:

The Owl, a Bird of Few Words, cursed the Pigeon for depriving him of a meal ...
The Owl decided to go in search of something substantial
Like a rabbit or a mole or a skunk.

■

"Under-Song For A Cipher" is substantial. There is an owl-like virtuosity to it, silent, unassuming—but deadly. Not yet forty, Yiadom-Boakye is a long way down the path to "mastry," and you do not doubt she will reach her destination. But the past two decades of art criticism have not been kind to formal mastery: it has been considered something inherently suspicious, a message sometimes too swiftly absorbed by artists themselves. From an essay on Yiadom-Boakye, "The Meaning of Restraint," by the French cultural critic Donatien Grau: "We can sense virtuosity in every inch of the artist's paintings, but it is always rather subdued, and never blatantly exposed. She makes the decision to not abandon herself in representational extravagance, to rather be discreet in the demonstration of her painterly capacity."

Those days are done: here is blatant virtuosity, hiding in plain sight, and the restraint has shifted to the narrative itself, which now offers us only as much as we might need to prompt our own creative projections—no more, no less. Many critics have noted that this return to "painterly capacity" is particularly notable in Black artists, and, strange indeed, that they should be the gateway—the permission needed—to return to the figurative, to the possibility of virtuosity! Why this might be the case is a fraught question, and Yiadom-Boakye, in her interview with Beckwith, proves herself slyly aware of its implications: "How many times have I heard from someone saying, 'You're lucky. You were born with a subject.' Well, isn't everyone?"

It's a familiar, backhanded compliment. *Blackness is in fashion—lucky you!* Implicit is the querulous ressentiment of the Skeptical Pigeon, who would be the type to come right out and say it: if these paintings were all of white people, would they have garnered the same attention, the same success? (In 2013, Yiadom-Boakye was short-listed for the Turner Prize, and in the past few years her paintings have begun to sell at auction for prices approaching seven hundred thousand dollars.) Well, the new has an aesthetic value, of this there is no doubt, and it's one that any smart artist is wise to exploit. But what Yiadom-Boakye does with brown paint and brown people is indivisible. Everyone is born with a subject, but it is fully expressed only through a commitment to form, and Yiadom-Boakye is as committed to her kaleidoscope of browns as Lucian Freud was to the veiny blues and the bruised, sickly yellows that it was his life's work to reveal, lurking under all that pink flesh. In his case, no one thought to separate form from content, and Yiadom-Boakye's work is, among other things, an attempt to insist on the same aesthetic unities that white artists take for granted.

"Under-Song For A Cipher." If it were a novel's title, we would submit it to textual analysis. *Undersong*: 1. A subordinate or subdued song or strain, esp. one serving as an accompaniment or burden to another. 2. An underlying meaning; an undertone. *Cipher*: 1. A person who fills a place, but is of no importance or worth, a nonentity, a "mere nothing." 2. A secret or disguised manner of writing, whether by characters arbitrarily invented, or by an arbitrary use of letters or characters in other than their ordinary sense. To these definitions, taken from the Oxford English Dictionary, I'd add the significance of "cipher" in hip-hop: a circle of rappers taking turns to freestyle over a beat. Then, with this knowledge in hand, I might turn to one Yiadom-Boakye painting in particular, "Mercy Over Matter," in which a man holds a bird on his finger. The undersong here is underplumage: those jewel-like greens and purples and reds you can spot beneath the oil-slick surface of certain black-feathered birds. The man's jacket magically displays this same underplumage; so does his skin; so does his bird. He is a Black man. He is often thought of as a nothing, a cipher. But he has layers upon layers upon layers.

Heidi Sopinka

Heidi Sopinka began her literary career by way of journalism; the one-time environment columnist for the *Globe and Mail*, she won a national magazine award in Canada, and has published essays in the *Believer* and the *Paris Review*. Sopinka's debut novel, *The Dictionary of Animal Languages* (2018), has an especially close relationship to the essay collected here—in both, Sopinka meditates on the work of Leonora Carrington (in the novel: through a roman-á-clef; in the essay: through a deeply reflective and closely related description of a journey). Every essay demonstrates a different version of turning to art for solace, repair, and redemption, but the most extreme drive to heal oneself with art is found in this essay, the second in this collection on Carrington. Years before she writes the essay, she traveled to Mexico City to find Carrington, who she thought could "help lead me out"—out "of the unsettling place between human and nonhuman, being and nonbeing," of "that dark, debilitating nothingness that causes our last and final disappearance" following the intense and nearly fatal illness of her newborn baby years earlier. Eventually knocking on the right door, Sopinka finds a Carrington willing to talk, but not to answer her question about death: "All the thinking you do, I doubt you'll figure out much." This refusal reveals its own kind of potency: "a decade and a novel later, I see what a ridiculous question I had posed. Who can possibly tell you about death?" In communion with Carrington, Sopinka finds that art pulls us away from oblivion. "It is the work itself that beats death, nothing else."

Hey, Necromancer!

What did we have on that day? We must have looked like maniacs. Striped long skirts and bracelets made from silver duct tape, dragging a leather suitcase that looked like the underbelly of a snake. We stood in front of a thick wooden door in the leafy Mexico City neighborhood of Roma, across from an enormous earthquake-collapsed building, overrun with cats and scorpions. I had come with two friends full of purpose—to make art, to find a death guide—and in the almost hallucinatory Mexican sun, we knocked on the door. After a good amount of time, the door swung open, and a moonfaced housekeeper named Yolanda told us in Spanish to come back in two days. Leonora, last of the living surrealists, wasn't well.

Four years earlier and six weeks too soon, I'd given birth to a baby. You might say my death drive, as Freud calls it, had made itself known. The baby's lungs weren't working properly, so he was hooked up to an incubator, and I was told to go home without him. It was a full moon. There were no beds, they said. I remember lying in our bedroom with my husband, a basket beside us but no baby in it. We would take a taxi to the hospital so that I could breastfeed, only to find that they'd just fed the baby through a tube in his nose. Because they kept bank hours, my husband and I were stuck waiting it out near the hospital between feedings. I remember sitting in a generic jazz bar thinking, My baby is in a plastic box in neonatal intensive care, and I am listening to a woman in a pantsuit belting out "My Way." I'd kept it in, the whole shock of the rapid premature birth, the worry for the baby, the separation, but this was the final blow. Everything was wrong. Tears streamed down. I couldn't stop crying.

And then, a week later, miraculously, he was in the basket. This simple arithmetic lodged in my brain. The cosmic joke: in birth, we appear; in death, we disappear. I became fixated on this, struck in particular by the metaphysical absurdity of death.

■

"He still has angels around him," a woman on a park bench told me, referring to the new baby. I wondered if I was hallucinating. She was wearing a belted wool coat, though we were in a heat wave. Mavis Gallant had wrecked angels for me when she said, "All angels are stupid," but I understood what the woman meant. He still had something of nowhere, of elsewhere, about him.

I began writing what Margaret Laurence called an "old lady" novel. I say "writing," but because of the intensity of early motherhood, it was more like a weird, hyperactive enterprise performed in stolen moments. That winter, I trudged through snow to the library, baby strapped to me, and ended up leaving with a slender purple novel by Leonora Carrington called *The Hearing Trumpet.* Darkly comic and apocalyptic, it has what we would now call an ecofeminist heroine who refuses to consider death. The book was written in the fifties and, among other things, tackles gender identity, terrestrial reorder, and psychic freedom. Oddly, like Carrington's novel, my draft had a ninety-two-year-old at its center too. When I looked up Carrington and saw that she was then ninety-two, it seemed too strange a coincidence to ignore.

It's easy to write off surrealism, with its puns, pipes, and bowler hats, but its strange, uncanny nature was born of deep traumatic shock post–World War I. After the violence of birth, I felt joltingly alive, the distressing kind of alive that has a bit of death in it. I was in the unsettling place between human and nonhuman, being and nonbeing—that dark, debilitating nothingness that causes our last and final disappearance. This is the place from which I came to Leonora, who referred to herself as a "female human animal," who made paintings that look like medieval pageant plays from another planet and gave them titles like *Aardvark Groomed by Widows* and *Who Art Thou, White Face?* I thought, through her deep-diving journeys inward, she might help lead me out. Her mind-blowing space-alien mix of the occult with old-world European esoterica and Mayan, Celtic, and Buddhist myth formed her own sharply focused vision. She had called forth the underworld, and I wanted, like Baudelaire, to call to her, Yo, necromancer.

Armed only with a telephone number copied down from the *páginas blancas*, I had flown to Mexico with two friends to hunt her down.

We called and called, and eventually, someone answered. It was a hair salon. With only a few more days left to make contact, we started to accept that we might never find her. Drinking tequila on the rooftop, we admitted to the French filmmaker we were staying with that we had no formal interview set up, no address. He seemed a bit horrified. But then, the next morning, he called us. "You're not going to believe this," he said, "but my ex-girlfriend lives on her street." So like a kind of lucid dream, in a city of twenty million people, we found her address.

Two days after Yolanda turned us away, Leonora herself answered the door. She stood ramrod straight, piled with sweaters, her blazing black eyes full of electricity. She was wraith thin and chain-smoking, and she carried a kind of unplaceable old-world aristocratic bearing, hair swept up, dressed for English weather. She let us into her house, where a tree grew through the center, in an inner garden. First we sat in her dark, chilly kitchen. She smoked Marlboros continuously, so we did too. It felt a bit like purgatory. "What do you want?" she kept asking, without ironic undertow, refusing to playact any artificiality. I wanted to know about death but thought better of beginning there, so I told her I was writing a novel about a ninety-two-year-old. She laughed, blowing out a stream of smoke. "It took me twenty years to find a publisher willing to touch a book about an elderly woman being shipped off to a home for senile females." I pointed out that her book was now a Penguin Classic, to which she countered: "One that has been out of print since the 1970s."

Death guides aren't born; they make themselves. Leonora Carrington was born into extreme wealth in England in 1917. She was expected to marry into the aristocracy, though it was clear, even from a young age, that she would outwit her destiny. She was deeply miserable at convent school, where she drew incessantly and smuggled in cigarettes, and she was kicked out for things such as writing backward and trying to levitate. She endured her own coming-out ball and then wrote about it. Where someone else might have simply satirized the experience, she shot it out of a cannon. Her short story "The Debutante" tells of a hyena she dresses up and sends in her place wearing the "very neatly nibbled all around" face of her recently murdered maid as a mask. At the end of the story, the hyena removes the human face and, to the horror of the dinner guests, eats it.

We are living in monstrous times. Leonora and the women of surrealism—such as Meret Oppenheim, Dora Maar, Toyen, and Maruja Mallo—had to outsmart male authority by engaging on different terms, creating their own female archetypes and their own freedoms. Now we have finally begun to see them as the contemporary feminist heroes they were. With her distinctly female vision of dark futures and wildly feminist weirdness, Carrington couldn't be more uncomfortably relevant. While we've just begun to talk about gender fluidity, she was already onto species fluidity. She advocated and rendered for us an androgynous, radical inclusivity that strikes the distinct tone of now. She saw us all on the same plane—humans, plants, animals, minerals. "Despise nothing, ignore nothing," she instructed, instructs us still.

On our second afternoon in her house, we walked up the stairs, past the tree, and into another dimension. Her sunny living room was filled with tapestries, sculptures, photographs by her friend Lee Miller, and drawings by Max Ernst, whom she'd met at a dinner party in London when she was barely twenty. He was forty-six and married to his second wife at the time, but the meeting struck them both with such force that she left everything she knew and ran away with him to Paris, where surrealism was in full cry. "You became a surrealist," I ventured. "I *was* a surrealist," Leonora corrected, saying it was the first time she ever felt, in her entire life, that she belonged.

With war at their heels, they fled south, and when Ernst was taken to an internment camp, she stopped eating, started drinking, and began to hallucinate. She felt like an animal; she felt like the universe (a combination that both describes her descent into madness and sounds an awful lot like childbirth). On the way to the coast, she ended up in an asylum in Spain. Newly released, Ernst arrived on their doorstep only to find she had vanished. He gathered up their paintings and fled to Lisbon, where by chance they found each other. She had escaped from the asylum and, in order to travel to America, married a Mexican poet friend of Picasso's. Ernst had become engaged to Peggy Guggenheim. In New York, Ernst—who, according to Guggenheim, was "still obsessed with the beautiful painter"—tried to win her back. But by this point, Carrington had transformed herself into something else. She had worked out an important truth about being a female artist: to be with a more famous man meant she would never get to be herself. They exchanged portraits of each other and never saw each other again. Decades later, she looks straight into a camera in Pamela Robertson-Pearce's documentary *Gifted Beauty* and says: "The soul is very important. You have to own your soul, as far as it's possible to own your soul—or for it to own you. But to give it over to some half-assed male? I wouldn't recommend it."

Her small white dog, Yeti, sat by her chair while she smoked the Marlboros we'd brought for her. She told us about the alchemical experiments she'd learned from female healers in the market and concocted in her kitchen with her close friend, the painter Remedios Varo. She'd lived in this house fifty years, with her two sons and second husband, a Hungarian photojournalist—whose ghost she said she occasionally saw smoking at the end of their table. In the top-floor studio, she had painted for almost seventy years, including posters in the seventies for Mexican women's liberation, pairing the saints and their miraculous actions with a feminist consciousness.

"We know nothing about death," she'd once said. "We've been brainwashed into the idea of death as horrible, disgusting, and shameful—and also the end. But the end of what? What is it the end of?"

When I finally told her I'd been thinking a lot about death, she cut me off in her droll upper-crust English, saying, "All the thinking you do, I doubt you'll figure out much."

She spoke of a lot of things—including her friend the surrealist Leonor Fini, who in Paris used to arrive at parties at midnight, cross-dressed or wearing nothing but white boots and a feather cape—but not death. Perhaps at ninety-two, she was too close to it now to philosophize. Or ever the rebel, she rejected the wise mentor role I wanted her to take.

Leonora refused the reality she was given and dream-lived her own, arrowing into hallucinations, darkness, and death. I was a new mother and a fledgling writer, between states, and something pulled me toward her frequency. But it was like looking for a guide on a trip where you're not allowed to take anything with you. In her presence, I saw that understanding death is like understanding life—a process that cannot be summed up. Its very definition is the disintegration of meaning.

I went home and immediately tore up my draft. I hadn't just met the last surrealist or someone of interest to me and my book. It felt more like discovering a lost planet, a once-in-a-millennium heavy hitter of rare, wild talent (even Picasso, after all, was a failed poet, whereas Carrington wrote and painted, literally, with both hands).

And now, a decade and a novel later, I see what a ridiculous question I had posed. Who can possibly tell you about death? She had no need to talk of it, especially when her painting and writing dragged it squarely into life. By refusing to answer me, she made me more present to myself. The revelation is within, to what you, as female human animal, are capable of. In the end, the book I wrote, *The Dictionary of Animal Languages*, is about an old woman. There is a lost child, a lost painting, a troubled affair, but at the heart of it, it is none of those things. It is a book about a woman working. Leonora took everything she knew and everything she couldn't and shaped it—into layers of egg tempera and hand-ground pigments, words, and political posters—and it became something else, something truthful and unsettlingly alive. Something immortal. She showed us what making art can do. It is the work itself that beats death, nothing else.

Hanya Yanagihara

Hanya Yanagihara is an American writer and editor. Author of 2013's *The People in the Trees*, Yanagihara's second novel, *A Little Life* (2015), drew serious critical attention for its multilayered and deeply affecting account of a group of college friends. Unlike many of her peers, Yanagihara entered the literary world through professional channels, moving from publicist at a number of publishing houses to journalist and editor with Conde Nast. She continues to edit *T: The New York Style Magazine*, where she argued in an editorial that, "for those of us who are *not* artists, our job is as important: to look and hear and listen with our whole hearts, to be vulnerable in the face of another's work, to be open to discomfort, to see ourselves in the lives of another. Art cannot save the world, but it isn't meant to—it is meant to ask what it means to be human, again and again, no matter the state of the world, no matter the cost." Her essay on the artist David Wojnarowicz, originally published in the exhibition catalogue *David Wojnarowicz: History Keeps Me Awake at Night* for a survey of his work at the Whitney Museum of American Art in 2018, follows through on this conviction; she admonishes the reader not to "ignore one of the essential teachings of his art, which is that throughout its short history, America has always hated some part of itself," while figuring the artist's works as a kind of suspended resource for the world, "waiting still, ready and tensed for when they might be needed next."

The Burning House

I was reading *Close to the Knives* in Mexico, where David Wojnarowicz spent significant amounts of time—Oaxaca, mainly, and Mexico City and the border towns—though I didn't know that then. I was staying at an expensive resort, which was in a state of constant repair, as those kinds of resorts always are: stucco was being smoothed and repainted, bright clouds of bougainvillea were being trimmed, concrete was being resurfaced. It was an ultimately futile tussle between man and nature, one frustrating and poignant to watch; it took teams of people, and their collective diligence, to try to undo what nature would keep doing. One day, the resort would close, and within months or weeks or days, all of those years of vigilance would mean nothing—the rains would rust the metal lanterns, the sun would leach the color from the walls, the hibiscus would grow stalky and shaggy.

I mention this because we tend to associate Wojnarowicz with a specific moment in the culture, with a particular movement of art, and with a brief span of years. On one hand, you can't not: his art was inextricable from his own biography. It was art that swept up the entirety of who the artist was and what he had experienced—and had seen and felt—into a single image and spat it back out at the viewer; there is a shimmering present-tenseness to it. My life flashed before my eyes, we say when we fear we have just only escaped death, and to look at his work is to realize how charged, how exhausting it must have been to live when your life was *always* flashing before your eyes, and not just your life but your friends' lives, and to be so overwhelmed by that constant blur of images, that whir that both never ended and that you prayed would never end.

And yet to associate Wojnarowicz with *only* those years (though that would be enough) would be to ignore one of the essential teachings of his art, which is that throughout its short history, America has always hated some part of itself. You could write a chronicle of this country by documenting which part of its population America has loathed and tried to disown at various points and why: Native Americans and women and Japanese Americans and Mexican immigrants and people with AIDS. Some groups—like Black people—America has always hated. But this self-hatred, this turning against our own, this disavowing of those we have hurt or harmed or those we might be able to help, is a curious and awful national impulse, as baked into our identity as our equally notable sense of generosity, our love of friendliness. All countries hate their own, of course, but what makes America's tendency so wounding to those of us who have been or are hated is its promise—which so many of us still believe and which the country depends on our believing—that it will behave otherwise, that it will be the exception, that it will not do what nations throughout history have always done. "These are strange and dangerous times," I read in an essay titled "In the Shadow of the American Dream." "Some of us are born with the cross hairs of a rifle scope printed on our backs or skulls. Sometimes it's a matter of thought, sometimes activity, and most times it's color." Wojnarowicz wrote those lines in the late eighties. But just five hundred miles north of where I lay watching a man in a stifling-looking tan uniform scrape a sun-seared gecko away from the pavement, there were policemen killing unarmed Black men, and political candidates announcing that we should turn away refugees from regions whose affairs we had injudiciously involved ourselves in—he could have written them now. When you accept that this is how your country operates, you will always be fearful: will I be next? "These are strange and dangerous times."

■

Close to the Knives: A Memoir of Disintegration was published in 1991, and while it's not Wojnarowicz's only book—there are also *Memories That Smell Like Gasoline* and *In the Shadow of the American Dream* and *Seven Miles a Second*—it's his best known and one of only three that were published before his death from an AIDS-related illness, at the age of thirty-seven, in 1992.

It's perhaps not surprising, given how many more artists are educated these days at graduate programs and how dedicated to one genre of art or another those programs typically are, that relatively few writers are also painters, or dancers are also photographers. Wojnarowicz was self-educated in almost everything in life—painting and stencil work and printmaking and photography and activism and sex—and in his writing, as in his artwork, you can feel the presence of someone for whom there is no fear of breaking the rules, because he has never been taught the rules to break. That ignorance is part of what gives the work its charge and confidence, its seethe and crackle.

When you look at Wojnarowicz's work, you are struck by how imperfect it is. We live in an era of technical perfection, of art that is beautifully presented and beautifully composed. In his prints, though, colors smudge outside the borders; you can actually watch, as in time-lapse, his photographs become more accomplished, less unintentionally grainy and more intentionally so. You have the sense, as a viewer, of both someone for whom time was on fire—and who was compelled to produce as much as possible, as quickly as possible because perfection and finesse demanded an extravagance of time that he didn't have—but also, more achingly, someone who was rapacious about his learning, for whom improvement was important (a very American quality, that). But there's also a thrilling sense of someone unable to edit himself even if he wanted to: unlike his colleagues and peers, Wojnarowicz couldn't hide his art's ferocity behind likability (like Keith Haring could) or cool wit (like Tseng Kwong Chi) or elegance (like Peter Hujar)—his work was his work.

In the same way, the writing is imperfect. It assaults the reader: to enter one of Wojnarowicz's texts, whether on the page or on the painting, is to be sucked immediately into its undertow, its incantatory, rushed, gloriously run-on sentences and breathless paragraphs, its made-up, jittery punctuations and scattershot capitalizations. It is impolite writing—impolite in its lack of structure, in its sudden, prefaceless glides between fantasy and reality, in its hyperactivity, in its lack of deference to the reader. But the work doesn't taunt: it's the difference between writing that says, Catch me if you can, and, Come with me, come with me, come with me. This writing wants you to follow it, and you want to follow it too.

Close to the Knives is subtitled and marketed as a memoir, and it sort of is, in the same way that all of Wojnarowicz's work might be subtitled and marketed as memoir: a collection of essays and speeches and dreams that circle between two poles, of anger and sorrow, like a crop duster buzzing an incessant loop over a smoldering swath of land. But really what it feels most like is what it in fact is: war reportage. The most similar experience I had to reading *Knives* is encountering Shomei Tomatsu's 1967 monograph *Nihon*. Tomatsu was one of Japan's greatest postwar artists, and his subject was the country's defeat and humiliation and eventual rebirth as a Westernized, modernized country. There is nothing in content or style that relates these two artists, and yet to look at Tomatsu's photographs—of almost-elderly Japanese women still wearing traditional dress, their hairpieces knocked askew and their makeup tawdry; of a middle-aged couple, clutching at some of their possessions, sitting slumped and unloved at the end of an alley, at the heel end of their stores of dignity—is to sense the same sort of rage, the same sort of awful privilege of getting to see and record suffering, the same sort of tenderness and love for those around you, for life itself, that makes living both unbearable and worthwhile, that you find on every page of *Knives*.

Because if rage is most of what motors *Knives*, it's not the only thing. In instance after instance, the prose becomes beautiful and loving, comes to *celebrate* beauty and loving. Sex is a confusion, something that was done to the ten-year-old Wojnarowicz; sex is something that makes him less than in his own country; and yet sex is also a source of ecstasy, both a release from and one of the fundamental pleasures of being alive: "In loving him, I saw great houses being erected that would soon slide into the waiting and stirring seas. I saw him freeing me from the silences of the interior life," he writes, in "Losing the Form in Darkness." In the writing, there is that yearning for what we all hope love will do: answer the silences that live within us, release us from the torment of being ourselves, remind us that what we are taught to think about ourselves is meaningless compared to what we can occasionally feel about ourselves.

Indeed, part of what makes Wojnarowicz's work so potent is how sincere it is. It reminds you that there is a distinction between cynicism and anger, because the work, while angry, is rarely bitter—bitterness is the absence of hope; anger is hope's companion. What you find instead, tucked like blossoms into the text, is real desire: for love, as I've said, but also for belonging. This fury of not belonging, of being rejected, isn't contextless; it is the fury of someone who wants, who *demands* to be counted as a full human being, who wants his life and his dying to mean something to his fellow Americans, who wants a price to be attached to his existence. In a country where some

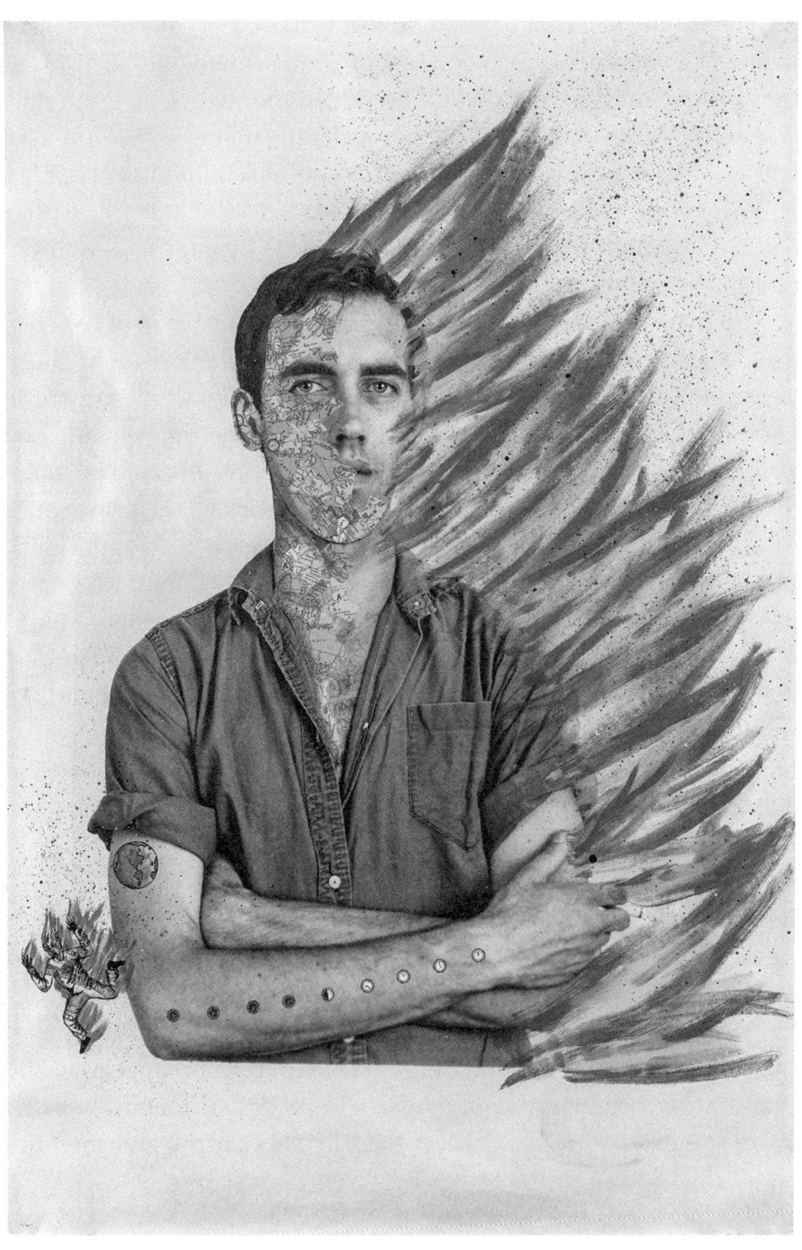

David Wojnarowicz and Tom Warren, *Portrait/Self Portrait of David Wojnarowicz*, 1983–84. Acrylic and collaged paper on gelatin silver print, 58½ x 39 inches. Collection of Brooke Garber Neidich and Daniel Neidich. Photograph by Ron Amstutz.

people are reviled, other people are valued, and Wojnarowicz's gall comes from his daring to have a sense of entitlement, his expectation that he, and all his tribe, should be valued too. It is such a humble, vulnerable wish—a child's wish: please let me matter—that it makes you want to cry. There is also his unloved child's habit of creating parents where none exist: Father Genet, Father Rimbaud, Father Mishima—ways of reassuring himself that he belongs to a family, a race of men who love other men.

And there is also in *Knives*, unexpectedly, a celebration of America itself, specifically the iconography of America—the long, long highways; the blue glow of the television; the roadside truck stops; the low-ceilinged motels; the orange-clay buttes; the truckers and the cowboys and the cops. It may be a sour celebration—the cops are there to beat you, the truck stops are where you get fucked, the television is where you see Jesse Helms saying you don't deserve to exist, the highways are what you traverse to get away from your father, who hates you, to a city where you can finally search for your own people—but it is impossible to read these chapters without recalling the iconography that Wojnarowicz invented for himself and spray-painted around the city like runes: if you can read this, you are one of us. The burning house, the target, the soldier with his gun, the flames, the clouds, the dancing man, the falling man—again and again, the falling man.

■

Recently, there's been a revival of interest in the years Wojnarowicz was working in New York, making his art, raging against those who reviled him and so many thousands of others for having AIDS and for being gay and for being inconvenient. New York in those years—from the late seventies, when the first cases of AIDS appeared, the gate-crasher bringing the giddy party to its end, through the naming of the disease by the Centers for Disease Control, and then the rapidly mounting death tolls—has been or will be the subject of novels and television shows and movies. There is at least one book being published that imagines Wojnarowicz's life in the city, and it's not difficult to see why and how, in the midst of this resurrection, Wojnarowicz might be irresistible: he was so young and so prolific and so vivid. He may have been ambivalent about the art world and its populace—"Susan Whatshername," he dismisses Sontag, writing about photography, and in the essay "Postcards from America": "The major museums in New York, not to mention museums around the country, are just as guilty of . . . selective cultural support and denial" as the government—but one can't help but wonder what he'd think of this New York, our New York, so close (and it is) and so far (and it is) from the one he inhabited. One wonders if he will become a piece of iconography himself, the kind that is pinned to a dorm-room wall, with only the face changing every decade: James Dean to Malcolm X to Jimi Hendrix to John Lennon to Steve Jobs.

And yet it's important not to romanticize either the era or the man because when you make a person into an icon, you stop seeing anything past the image itself. A weariness of looking sets in: every movement in America has its own totems, and it's easy enough, in this age, to shorthand our way through history, to assume that recognizing the symbol—the fold of red ribbon, the hot-pink triangle, the hooded sweatshirt, the multicolored flag—means understanding the narrative behind it. When we make artists into martyrs, we stop their movement and affix them to a sheet of paper, rendering them immobile. We can't help ourselves; it happens so easily, and we are always looking for people to love, even difficult people. But it doesn't help us understand them any more clearly.

It's equally easy to fathom what might have inspired this renewal of fascination for New York during its most inequitable, most desperate, most death-filled years in modern times: what we crave is that sense of collective movement, of collective uncertainty, that sense that nothing, not gender or sexuality or money, could insulate you from something large and immediate and terrifying that could yet shrink itself into something so tiny that it could wriggle in through the walls of your building, past your sheets, and into your blood; that sensation that life was quavering and temporal, that you had to be vigilant, even while completing the most mundane tasks of life. Now that seems exotic and bracing. Then, the war wasn't someplace far off, something you could turn off or ignore or dip into only when you were feeling guilty; it was two miles south of you, it was seven blocks east, it was one door down. For years, AIDS stratified the city; it drained it of compassion. Like all plagues, it segregated and categorized. But if you lived in the city, you had no choice but to contend with its existence. If you arranged your life just so, you might be able to avoid thinking about it, but you weren't able to deny it.

In America, we are consumed with the idea of happiness. It's our birthright, this promise, and so much of our lives is spent in pursuit of it that the quest can become oppressive (not to mention ridiculous: so many of us can't define it and yet are told to want it, which is the equivalent of running a race on a road that doubles back on itself without our noticing). But really, this country has always been at its best when it is angry, and what really makes us American is not the right to happiness but our right to be angry, to shout and protest without fear of reprisal, to know that even if we are a member of the most hated group in this country, it is our right to try to be heard. Maybe what we're all yearning for is the blood-zinging fervor of being angry together, of feeling that there is something so urgent that it can't be ignored, of feeling something so huge that it blots out logic and good manners and good taste. "I wished I had a motorcycle and that I was in a faraway landscape, maybe someplace out west," Wojnarowicz writes in the fever-essay "In the Shadow of the American Dream."

> I saw myself riding this machine faster and faster and faster toward the edge of the cliff until I hit the right speed that would take me off the cliff in an arcing motion. At that instant when my body and the machine cleared the edge of the cliff and hit the point in the sky where I was neither rising nor falling—somewhere in there: once my body and the motorcycle hit a point in the light and wind and loss of gravity, in that exact moment, I would suddenly disappear, and the motorcycle would continue the downward arc of gravity and explode into flames somewhere among the rocks at the bottom of the cliff.

I love this passage because it, like so many of Wojnarowicz's creations, captures another key element of Americanness: the need for velocity, to feel ourselves being propelled through space, imagining we have the ability to outrun anything that might be pursuing us, that we can make it out of the burning house with not just the one thing most precious to us—but everything.

■

I have said it's important not to romanticize, and it is. But as I was reading, I kept thinking of a fable I had loved as a child. "The Boy Who Drew Cats" is a Japanese folktale, recorded, altered, and published by the literary anthropologist Lafcadio Hearn in 1898. The story is about a boy who grows up in a family of farmers, but instead of performing his tasks, he wants only to draw—specifically, to draw cats. He is talented, but there is no money for school, and art isn't even a dream; it is an impossibility. His father, frustrated, gives the boy to a local temple as an acolyte, but here, too, he is rejected: he is dreamy and unfocused and unable to do anything but draw cats.

The night he is to be cast out of the monastery, the abbot gives him some food and some advice: "Avoid large places; keep to small." And with only these kindnesses, so stingy they are hardly kindnesses at all, the boy leaves. He walks and walks. He should be frightened, and perhaps he is—Japan at night is full of goblins, the hills busy with demons—but no mention is ever made of how the boy feels on this journey, on being discarded for a second time. Finally, after many miles, he is exhausted, and when he sees a temple, high on a hill, he climbs toward it. The boy calls out, but no one answers, and finally, he lets himself into the empty building.

What the boy doesn't know is that the temple has been abandoned because it has become the haunt of a goblin, one that not even the monks can expel. Here, Hearn tells us, he is frightened, but it is dark, and there is nowhere for him to go. To comfort himself, he finds some ink and begins to draw: over the rice-paper walls, across the tatami-mat floors, up and down the wooden beams. Again and again, he paints cats, so many that soon the room is covered. But before he goes to sleep, he remembers the abbot's warning—avoid large places; keep to small—and tucks himself into a cupboard.

Late that night, he wakes to a terrible noise: a screeching, a wailing, a tearing of flesh, a splatter of liquid on straw, a rending, a ripping—Hearn does not specify. The boy hears bone cracking against bone, hears the wet thwack of meat being slammed against a hard surface, hears the clamorous sound of death and suffering. He tucks himself tighter into the corner of the cupboard and waits. On and on the horror goes; on and on he waits. And then, abruptly, it stops. He waits and waits some more. And then, at last, he draws back the cupboard's sliding door and steps out. There he sees, in the middle of the room, a rat. A goblin rat. A goblin rat so enormous that for a while, its exact shape is unclear: the boy sees only a hill of bloody fat and flesh, not its actual form. And then he looks around him and sees his cats and sees that all of their mouths are wet and red and realizes that his creations have killed what others, in their inability to conquer, have run from.

After that, Hearn tells us, the boy becomes a hero and, later, a great artist. "The Boy Who Drew Cats" is meant as a ghost story, but it is really a fable of transformation, the one every artist has at some point hoped for: that someday, his art will do what not only he cannot but what no one can. It will come to life, golemlike, and it will save him, it will protect him, it will avenge him. One day, this kid will get larger, and he will destroy everyone who tried to push him down or away, who hid him in a cupboard.

Perhaps that hope burns doubly high when what you want to be avenged for is the right to love and fuck who you want. Perhaps it is doubly charged when it is driven by the belief that eventually sheer relentlessness will save you, that if you say it enough, if you draw it not once but hundreds of times, thousands of times, the America you want to exist will materialize before you, its atoms rearranging themselves to create a picture you don't yet know how to imagine.

Maybe Wojnarowicz saw all this. Probably he didn't. But I like to think that he would have liked to see all these symbols, his own versions of cats, here in one place, an army of his own fighters that have long outlived not only him but so many of his friends and members of his tribe. All this iconography drawn not across a temple's walls but across his own version of a temple, New York, the place he came to, as so many have and so many will, when no place else felt like home: on the walls of the Hudson Piers and the Second Avenue subway stop, on the sidewalks of the East Village, and on the backs of already-used pieces of paper collected in his apartment. Hundreds of them, a militia of orphans: burning house, falling man, target. Soldier, dancing man, America in flames. So many that even after the goblin is killed, they're waiting still, ready and tensed for when they might be needed next.

Permissions

"A Leonora Carrington A to Z," from *London Review of Books Blog*, April 6, 2017, by Chloe Aridjis. Copyright © Chloe Aridjis, 2017. Reprinted by permission of the author.

"You Need to Look Away: Visions of Contemporary Malaysia," from *The Weeklings*, April 4, 2014, by Tash Aw. Copyright © Tash Aw, 2014. Reprinted by permission of the author c/o The Wylie Agency, 17 Bedford Square, London WC1B 3JA.

"How Paint and Perception Collide in the Work of Late Surrealist Dorothea Tanning," from *Fish Out of Water*, by Claire-Louise Bennett. Copyright © Claire-Louise Bennett, 2020. Reprinted by permission of the author.

"There's Less to Portraits Than Meets the Eye, and More," from *New York Times Magazine*, August 23, 2018, by Teju Cole. Copyright © Teju Cole, 2018. Reprinted by permission of the author.

"Now We Can See," from *Dayanita Singh: Go Away Closer*, by Geoff Dyer. Copyright © Geoff Dyer, 2013. Reprinted by permission of the author c/o The Wylie Agency, 17 Bedford Square, London WC1B 3JA.

"Should Artists Shop or Stop Shopping?," from *Affidavit*, May 21, 2018, by Sheila Heti. Copyright © Sheila Heti, 2018. Reprinted by permission of the author c/o Sterling Lord Literistic, 115 Broadway, Suite 1602, New York, NY 10006.

"The Hunger," from *Frieze*, June 16, 2013, by Katie Kitamura. Copyright © Katie Kitamura, 2013. Reprinted by permission of the author c/o Trident Media Group, 355 Lexington Avenue, 12th Floor, New York, NY 10017.

"A Walk around the Neighborhood," from *Social Practices*, by Chris Kraus. Copyright © Chris Kraus, 2005. Reprinted by permission of the author.

"The Space between the Pictures," from *The Suspension of Time: Reflections on Simon Dinnerstein and The Fulbright Triptych*, by Jhumpa Lahiri. Copyright © Jhumpa Lahiri, 2011. Reprinted by permission of the author c/o WME, 11 Madison Avenue, New York, NY 10010.

"Damage Control," from *Harpers*, December 2013, by Ben Lerner. Copyright © Ben Lerner, 2013. Reprinted by permission of the author c/o ICM Partners, 65 E. 55th Street, New York, NY 10022.

"When Orhan Pamuk Met Anselm Kiefer," from the *Guardian*, April 25, 2015, by Orhan Pamuk. Copyright © Orhan Pamuk, 2015. Reprinted by permission of the author c/o The Wylie Agency, 17 Bedford Square, London WC1B 3JA.

"We Must Not Be Isolated," from *Frieze*, October 10, 2015, by Ali Smith. Copyright © Ali Smith, 2015. Reprinted by permission of the author, c/o RCW Literary Agency, 20 Powis Mews, London W11 1JN.

"Lynette Yiadom-Boakye's Imaginary Portraits," from *New Yorker*, June 12, 2017, by Zadie Smith. Copyright © Zadie Smith, 2017. Reprinted by permission of the author, c/o RCW Literary Agency, 20 Powis Mews, London W11 1JN.

"Hey, Necromancer!" from *Paris Review*, September 18, 2018, by Heidi Sopinka. Copyright © Heidi Sopinka, 2018. Reprinted by permission of the author.

"The Burning House," from *Paris Review*, July 2, 2018, by Hanya Yanagihara. Copyright © Hanya Yanagihara, 2018. Reprinted by permission of the author c/o ICM Partners, 65 E. 55th Street, New York, NY 10022.

The New American Canon

Half a Million Strong: Crowds and Power from Woodstock to Coachella
by Gina Arnold

Violet America: Regional Cosmopolitanism in U.S. Fiction since the Great Depression
by Jason Arthur

The Meanings of J. Robert Oppenheimer
by Lindsey Michael Banco

Neocolonial Fictions of the Global Cold War
edited by Steven Belletto and Joseph Keith

Workshops of Empire: Stegner, Engle, and American Creative Writing during the Cold War
by Eric Bennett

Places in the Making: A Cultural Geography of American Poetry
by Jim Cocola

The Legacy of David Foster Wallace
edited by Samuel Cohen and Lee Konstantinou

Race Sounds: The Art of Listening in African American Literature
by Nicole Brittingham Furlonge

Postmodern/Postwar—and After: Rethinking American Literature
edited by Jason Gladstone, Andrew Hoberek, and Daniel Worden

After the Program Era: The Past, Present, and Future of Creative Writing in the University
edited by Loren Glass

Hope Isn't Stupid: Utopian Affects in Contemporary American Literature
by Sean Austin Grattan

It's Just the Normal Noises: Marcus, Guralnick, No Depression, *and the Mystery of Americana Music*
by Timothy Gray

Wrong: A Critical Biography of Dennis Cooper
by Diarmuid Hester

Reverse Colonization: Science Fiction, Imperial Fantasy, and Alt-victimhood
by David M. Higgins

Art Essays: A Collection
edited by Alexandra Kingston-Reese

Contemporary Novelists and the Aesthetics of Twenty-First Century American Life
by Alexandra Kingston-Reese

American Unexceptionalism: The Everyman and the Suburban Novel after 9/11
by Kathy Knapp

Visible Dissent: Latin American Writers, Small U.S. Presses, and Progressive Social Change
by Teresa V. Longo

Pynchon's California
edited by Scott McClintock and John Miller

Richard Ford and the Ends of Realism
by Ian McGuire

Novel Subjects: Authorship as Radical Self-Care in Multiethnic American Narratives
by Leah A. Milnes

William Gibson and the Futures of Contemporary Culture
edited by Mitch R. Murray and Mathias Nilges

Poems of the American Empire: The Lyric Form in the Long Twentieth Century
by Jen Hedler Phillis

Reading Capitalist Realism
edited by Alison Shonkwiler and Leigh Claire La Berge

Technomodern Poetics: The American Literary Avant-Garde at the Start of the Information Age
by Todd F. Tietchen

Ecospatiality: A Place-Based Approach to American Literature
by Lowell Wyse

How to Revise a True War Story: Tim O'Brien's Process of Textual Production
by John K. Young